The road to
incorporation

By Ann Limb, John Avery,
Peter Briggs, Margaret Jack,
Colin Monk, John Skitt,
Paul Sokoloff and Jeremy Wilson

ISBN 0-907659-80-2

Published by The Staff College and the Association of Colleges for Further and Higher Education (ACFHE)

The Staff College
Coombe Lodge
Blagdon
Bristol BS18 6RG

Association of Colleges for Further and Higher Education
Swindon College
Regents Circus
Swindon
Wilts SN1 1PT

Commissioning Editor Ann Limb, Milton Keynes College
Cover design by Susan Leather, The Staff College
Layout and sub-editing by Pippa Toogood, The Staff College

Typesetting by Avonset, Midsomer Norton
Printed in the UK by Dotesios, Trowbridge

Contents

About the authors

Ann Limb

Ann Limb was born in Manchester in 1953 and is a teacher-trained modern linguist who has experience of teaching in secondary, further and community education in the United Kingdom and France. She holds degrees from the universities of Liverpool and Nancy, France, and a Diploma in Management Studies from Sheffield Polytechnic.

She began her career in further education in 1977 as a part-time lecturer. She taught in several further education and community colleges in Manchester and Derbyshire, becoming Head of Department of Management and Business Studies at North East Derbyshire College in 1985.

She has worked in industry as an interpreter/translator for the Merseyside Training Council and for a major construction company. She recently completed an industrial secondment working in the Government Services division of the management consultants Coopers and Lybrand. She has published numerous articles, papers and two books concerned with language learning. She is a member of the Languages Lead Body, the Board of Management of the Further Education Unit, and the DES Expert Committee on the Environment. She is also a member of the Electricity Consumer Council, and sits on the management committees of the Milton Keynes Citizens Advice Bureau and the Council of Voluntary Organisations.

Since 1989, she has been Director of Milton Keynes College.

John Avery

John Avery is Head of Estate Management at the Higher Education Funding Council for England, having been Head of Property Services at the Polytechnics and Colleges Funding Council, where much of his time in the past two years has been spent in developing with polytechnics and colleges a strategic view of estate management.

John was formerly Property Director at the Education Assets Board, having previously been in private practice and industry as a chartered surveyor, most recently as Managing Director of Thameside Properties Ltd, the property-owning subsidiary of the Brooke Bond Group.

Peter Briggs BA (Hons.) IPFA

Peter Briggs is currently Principal Finance Officer at Leeds Polytechnic where he has been in post since November 1988. He studied Economics, Accountancy and Law at Lancaster University and began working with the finance department of Leeds City Council in 1980, where he qualified as an accountant, and spent the majority of his time working on social services and education finance. In 1986 he took up the post of Senior Finance Officer in the Directorate of Educational Services at the City of Bradford Metropolitan Council where he worked for two years prior to moving to Leeds Polytechnic.

At Leeds Polytechnic Peter has specific responsibility for all financial and management accounting together with the use and development of financial systems. He handles the polytechnic's corporation tax and VAT matters and is responsible for updating the institution's financial procedures. For the first 18 months of corporate status he was also responsible for the investment of the polytechnic's surplus cash balances.

Margaret Jack

Margaret Jack joined BTEC as Director, Quality Assurance and Control in 1989, where she is responsible for the approval and ongoing monitoring of all BTEC programmes. She was formerly Deputy Director, Programmes at the PCFC and Assistant Secretary (Academic) at NAB, where she advised on the academic aspects of the planning and funding of higher education. Prior to that she was Deputy Academic Registrar at South Bank Polytechnic.

Her interest in quality is education developed from her earlier work on quality from a manufacturing perspective. She has a first degree in Industrial Engineering and Management and spent the early years of her career as a production engineer for Marks and Spencer where quality is of overriding importance.

She is currently a member of the steering group for a major research project on quality in higher education, government and employers. She is also a member of the FEFC working party on a funding methodology for the new FE sector.

Colin Monk

Colin Monk is currently Vice President (Commercial Services) at Portsmouth Polytechnic. He received a degree in Chemistry from Kings College, University of London and worked initially for Esso Petroleum Company Ltd. He then moved to America where he received a Masters in Business Administration (MBA) from Stamford University. Following this he joined an American multinational health care company and worked in the international division initially in the United States and then in Brazil and France. He returned to England in 1986 to start up the European business of a new technology company specialising in industrial filtration. He raised the capital for this company and built its European operations. During this time he was invited to serve on the board of governors at Ealing College. This experience showed him the immense potential in the area of education management, particularly with the new freedom and responsibility brought about by incorporation. It was this experience that led him to shift his career into full-time education management. He was a governor at Ealing College from 1988 until 1991.

John Skitt

John Skitt is currently Principal of Barnet College. He has been principal there since 1985. His previous experience has been with Luton College of Higher Education, Barnfield College and Middlesex University. In 1975 he published **Practical corporate planning in local government**. He holds a BA and an MA from Lancaster University.

A main concern of his has been to support the professional development of staff. John participated in the development of Barnet College's staff development, training and review policies since the early '80s. Barnet College's review and appraisal schemes have been used as a model both in the UK and abroad. In recent years these policies have been developed in the context of a whole college personnel policy.

John is active in promoting a unified voice for further education and in advocating a strong association of colleges. He is keen to internationalise FE in both curricular terms and in the sharing of practice and experience.

Paul Sokoloff

A biochemist by training, Paul Sokoloff began his career as a researcher in protozoology and immunobiology at the Wellcome Laboratories of Tropical Medicine, later moving into teaching and spending 15 years at the 'chalkface' lecturing in biochemistry and cell biology. During this time Paul became involved with the Technician Education Council (TEC), and later BTEC, as a moderator and part-time adviser to the science board. He joined BTEC's full-time staff in 1987 as an education adviser for assessment, later moving to manage a newly created monitoring department, developing statistical and other probes for examining the quality of assessment.

Paul is currently manager of BTEC's Validation Department and responsible for the front end quality control of all BTEC programmes. He has a keen interest in quality systems within institutions and has been at the forefront of development in review and evaluation, franchising and accreditation of prior learning.

Jeremy Wilson

Jeremy Wilson, a partner of Grimley J R Eve, Property Consultants, has a national responsibility for providing property advice to the further and higher education sector.

Jeremy is a Fellow of the Royal Institution of Chartered Surveyors in the Planning and Development division and is also a chartered town planner.

Jeremy heads a specialised team of surveyors and consultants within Grimley JR Eve who have gained substantial experience of the education sector from working with almost 30 PCFC institutions over the last four years.

Jeremy has spoken at numerous seminars and conferences on strategic property issues within the post-16 education sector. Specifically, Grimley J R Eve has recently concluded a sector-wide survey of the university's space capacity and accommodation needs which will contribute towards the formulation of estates policy for the new Higher Education Funding Council.

Introduction

Ann Limb
Principal
Milton Keynes College

As this book goes to press, most colleges designated by Act of Parliament to become further education corporations on 1 April 1993 are in the throes of detailed and time-consuming preparation for incorporation. With less than a year to go before colleges become independent organisations, we find ourselves on a road, if not less travelled, at the very least, comparatively short. The time needed to put in place, adequately and effectively, the strategies, structures, systems and staffing highlighted in the following chapters of this book, is limited.

Fortunately, for most professional educators, working in an environment which requires fast learning, quick action and careful application, is not new. As learners ourselves, concerned with the business of learning for some 3 million citizens in the United Kingdom, we, as teachers, managers and leaders in the further education service, have been encouraged to develop an understanding of the attitude and aptitudes needed to respond effectively to change.

Our separate and collective responses to this particular change are likely to be as varied as the sector itself. In time, it may be that our individual college and overall sector performance will reflect this diversity. Until the Further and Higher Education Act is implemented in full, through the new further education corporations, we will not be able to make an assessment of this.

Our task now is to address immediate preparation and implementation issues in a constructive and effective manner. This is the purpose of this book, conceived, designed and written to help guide college governors, chief executives and managers on their journey towards incorporation.

Chapter 1: College governance – the management responsibility

Colin Monk
Vice-President (Commercial Services)
Portsmouth Polytechnic

Preface

The changes taking place in further and higher education are dramatic and irreversible. Included is the requirement for hundreds of new governors, independent from the college, to take on a new and responsible duty. The responsibility of the further education college governor under the Further and Higher Education Act 1992 appears to be less clear cut than that of private sector directors who are covered by the Companies Act. The world of education management is often a strange and mysterious one to people who might become independent governors even though they have been the product of that same education system.

This section is written for two audiences. Firstly, the new FE college governor who takes on new and challenging responsibilities following incorporation and secondly, principals, chairs and members of formation committees having responsibility for forming the team of new governors that will guide their college into the uncharted waters of incorporation.

Introduction

Prisons have governors, Victorian children often had governors and governesses and indeed, until recently, polytechnics had governors. But it is a strange word that we use to describe one of the more responsible positions in the incorporated public sector world of both polytechnics and now, colleges of further and higher education. It is sad that we choose a word that invokes in most people these thoughts or even those of their earlier education where governors sat on the raised stage at speech day and beamed down at the graduating class with a quizzical pride. In fact the governor is a member of the board of directors. Governors have substantial responsibilities and will I hope, through the correct choice and perhaps even the reading of this chapter, take an active role in the direction of the college for which they are responsible.

Incorporation of colleges of further education is a major change in the landscape of education in the United Kingdom. When the polytechnics and many of the colleges of higher education were incorporated in 1989 following the 1988 Education Reform Act, some 83 higher education corporations were formed. However, with further education the total will be in excess of 600. This puts immense pressure on finding those people who are willing to act as governors in this situation and have the appropriate qualifications and attitude to education management. The college principals and chairs of formation committees will have to work extremely hard to put together an effective team.

This chapter is intended to help not only the new governors themselves but the principal and chair in understanding exactly what is the role of the independent governor. There should be a clear agreement of this role before embarking on the search for the people to fill it, for as we know, mistakes made at this level can often be costly and take many years to change.

So, it is important to look at the role of the governor, which I intend to do from the point of view of management responsibility. A document published in 1991 by the PCFC (**Guide for governors. Polytechnics and colleges of higher education** PCFC 1991) sets out some of the legal and constitutional issues of college governance and should be reviewed in detail.

The first part of this chapter will focus on the particular points that I believe are crucial to the new governors in their function as responsible managers. It is an attempt to make their lives easier during the first years as they find their way in these new and exciting jobs. I end this section by identifying what I would suggest as the appropriate governors' survival kit and then move on to draw some guidelines that may help principals and chairs in selecting governors for these new boards.

The chapter ends with a review of what I see as some of the challenges facing the current system of governance.

Differences beween management in education and the private sector

Many of the new governors will come from the private sector, as indeed I did in my first experience with Ealing College. There is a widely held belief that the management of education is similar to that of private sector management with the product being of an educational nature. And because it has been part of the traditional public sector in the past it is therefore just waiting for improvement by using standard private sector techniques. While there is a certain truth in these statements there are many fundamental differences between the public and the private sector that are not at first obvious and a clear understanding of these will make the new independent governor a more effective and perhaps even a humbler person.

The uniformly high intelligence of the workforce is a surprise – a pleasant surprise, but one that needs to be carefully understood. The danger is to talk down to people or to oversimplify issues. The governor has to be exceptionally well prepared for any contact with members of staff. They in turn expect nothing less than well constructed arguments and will quickly find out poorly formulated ideas or fuzzy logic.

The history of education management is that of slow consensus and involvement at all levels. There are strong similarities with Japanese management. Ideas are generated from the senior management group within the college and tested on respective groups of colleagues, either by faculty, department or area. Comments are incorporated in the final proposals which, although taking longer to prepare, are often more quickly implemented because of the degree of involvement at all levels. Private sector management does not function in this way although it is increasingly moving in this direction. Decisions are made by people who have responsibility and then are communicated down the line for action. Confidentiality is a crucial issue, sometimes for the right reason, e.g. specific company know-how and trade secrets and sometimes for the wrong reason, e.g. not wanting to have people discussing ideas before they are enacted.

In education as in other parts of the public sector, there is a deep sense of commitment to the core business. The motivation of employees by their belief in their role overcomes any act of management. If the average private sector company could have this degree of commitment throughout its workforce it would gain superior results. This sense of commitment and loyalty has to be carefully handled by the outsider as he/she realises its depth, otherwise it will be easy to offend or send the wrong messages about the governor's involvement.

There are few, if any, role models in education or education management. In the private sector there are many, even if some are bordering on the folk hero status. Similarly people identify with a profession such as engineering, accountancy or the law but in education the commitment is to the discipline and not the management of the discipline. This means that there is little transfer of best practice in the management sense either between colleagues or from, for example, the private sector.

Change is intensely threatening, particularly sudden change. The product life cycle of a particular course is measured in years. Minor changes occur across terms. To institute a new course and have it tested, approved and validated may take from four to five years. To be successful following incorporation many swift changes will be required. This will be threatening. Because of the resistance to change and, in fairness, the lack of experience in managing change, additional steps must be taken to ensure success. These come down to communication but the key, I believe, is that communication must come from all levels in the college and not just that of the immediate supervisor. Change will not result from an instruction; it comes from the total shift of the culture and that must involve everyone at every level.

Within education management there is little experience in target setting, appraisals, rewards or even penalties. These are seen as the attributes of the worst parts of the private sector. However, many of these procedures are becoming increasingly common in educational establishments, particularly target setting and staff appraisal; again they are very threatening to all individuals and a base must be carefully established with consultation if the change is to be successful.

I believe the most significant difference which is rarely discussed is that there is no common decision-making model in education. In the private sector money is used to distinguish between different programmes within a division and to distinguish between the performance and investment in different divisions within the same company. Investors will distinguish between different companies using objective numerical methods. Thus everything is reduced to numbers for most of the major decisions between competing alternatives. In education that is not so; there is no model. If a principal is faced with programmes competing for the same capital, how is the decision made? Not as easily as in the private sector and often the methods used cause resentment because one group cannot see why another group have received apparently favourable treatment. The answer here is the mission statement of the institution which must be more specific so as to offer the guidance on how scarce resources are allocated. Historically mission statements have not been used in this way and will be discussed in more detail under the heading 'ownership of the vision'.

The cheerleader

The governors must be the biggest supporters of the senior management group. If not, they should remove the senior management group and replace them with people they can support. Historically governors have been shadowy individuals who would arrive late in the day and leave even later having had little contact with the institution or indeed the senior management.

Anyone who has managed at the highest level in an organisation understands that it is, indeed, lonely at the top. The board of governors has the responsibility for the direction and ultimate survival of the college. The governors must support their management group from a motivational point of view in a similar fashion to any supervisor supporting his own staff. I believe that in addition the governors must help emphasise the senior management team's message, particularly as so much basic change will be required in the sector. They cannot communicate only through the senior management group. They must find ways and means of communicating directly with staff, students and the local community. The objective is to emphasise that they, the board of governors, in conjunction with the senior educational management team speak with a united voice on the major issues affecting the college. If this is not understood clearly, it will be more difficult to unite the staff in making the changes necessary for the future development of the college.

In being the cheerleaders of the institution the governors must show a certain degree of passion for the college and its place in the educational world. I am convinced that becoming a governor of a college is more an act of faith and less a decision of logic. Showing this openly does help provide the backdrop for change and give the confidence that the senior management team is in control.

Ownership of the vision

The most important management task of the governing body is to take ownership of the vision of the future direction of the college. The vision can be established by asking where is the institution going? Why is it going in that direction? and how can the college get there? This is, I believe, extremely important in the world of further education which, because of its multiplicity of contacts in the community and between other colleges, exists in a more complex environment – with many choices which need to be carefully understood in order to reach the correct strategic decision.

Two stories serve to illustrate this point. One may be somewhat mythical but it makes the point. A company in the early 1950s had built up a certain market in providing mechanical adding machines. They had successfully gained a major position in this market and were extremely profitable. However, a visionary chief executive lead the company in a short period of time to agree that they were in the business, not of making machines for a particular market, but of information and information management. That should be their main mission. That company went on to become IBM.

On a lesser scale but an example that I am more familiar with, Ealing College upon incorporation in 1989 quickly came to the conclusion that because of its size and relative position in the marketplace its major direction must be to seek polytechnic status as soon as was practical. By not doing so it would be forced into a merger with someone else. There followed a period of intense activity with several discussions that came to nothing. However, in 1991 within a six month period Ealing College merged with Thames Valley College of Higher Education, took over the Queen Charlotte School of Nursing and became the new home for the London College of Music. Several months later it was granted polytechnic status and will now become a university.

In the discussion and understanding of the vision, the governors must comprehend enough detail to understand the mission but avoid the use of detail in communicating that mission throughout the college. I have seen many mission statements which fill pages and pages. Many committees have been involved. However, no one individual can ever remember what the mission is nor can they be certain if they have done anything that day to contribute to its achievement. As an alternative I would offer the style contained in the mission statement of Humberside Polytechnic (now the University of Humberside).

> To become an enterprising, accessible and highly regarded polytechnic with a strong European and regional orientation and 8000 satisfied students. (University of Humberside mission statement.)

If you were a governor of the University of Humberside , you could remember that mission statement and it would permeate your thinking throughout each governors' meeting. Similarly managers and staff could go home at the end of each day and review whether they contributed to the mission statement that day.

So preparation and more importantly, ownership of the vision is crucially important to the successful board of governors as is the onward communication of that mission in the college and the community.

Monitor of change

There is an old saying, whose origin is lost in the mists of time, 'Never try to teach a pig to sing, it wastes your time and it annoys the pig'.

There is no intentional analogy in this statement other than to offer the thought that change is an intensely difficult subject to manage but it is of crucial importance, particularly for the institution approaching and immediately following incorporation and is probably the other most important issue the governors will face.

Governors must monitor change, not manage it. They cannot manage, nor will they understand, all of the detail but they must monitor its progress. By doing this they can often add value based on their own experiences of managing change, whether it is pushing a too reticent senior management team, or pulling them back if they are too headstrong. Governors will recognise some of the communication blockages that occur when changes are discussed in large organisations. It is this recognition that change is threatening and that support must be provided to result in effective change, that the governors must monitor.

The best method I can offer here is the use of milestones. Within every change programme, the senior manager responsible should present the milestones that he/she intends to reach and when they will be achieved, then report back to the governors on performance. Only in that way can the governors monitor how successfully the change is being implemented.

No change has ever been implemented successfully without some casualties. Private sector governors will understand this. There will always be people who are unable to change and the governors must help the institution recognise this and make sure that there are alternative plans in place that provide an honourable exit for the individuals concerned. Good human resource management understands that the clearest message sent to staff is always based on the treatment of other staff who are leaving.

The team player

Governors must understand that within the confidentiality of the governors' meeting they can argue and contest points of view but at the end they must all support the consensus of opinion-whether or not they actually agree with it personally. Independent governors will most likely come from a background that emphasises team support and development. However other governors come from different groups within the college structure and this may be a new concept to them which they will have to review carefully.

The Education Reform Act 1988 is quite clear in stating that governors are not representatives but come to the table as individuals with clearly different experiences but who can function as individuals within the responsibilities of the Act. This understanding must be clear or progress can be difficult. If after each decision a group of governors go forth and explain the detail of the decision and how close it was to being overturned (for example) then the position of the board will be undermined. All governors must be team players.

The watchdog

How does the governor whose knowledge of education is growing slowly and yet who has substantial fiduciary responsibility under the Acts of Parliament guarantee that the college is not heading for a disaster? There are two aspects that must be considered which will be more important in committees than in the main governors meeting. The first is that of demanding delegation. Representative governors on each committee must forcefully demand reports to show that their delegated authority is being used within the objectives and overall mission statement of the college. They cannot do the job themselves nor are they expected to but they can create this watchdog mentality such that the senior management feel supported in their demands within their own organisations for similar tight controls.

The other feature is that of forceful humility. Indeed many times a governor will not know the exact *modus operandi* of the college but his/her innate business sense will tell him or her that there is an issue that must be unearthed. This can best be discovered by recognising quite openly the lack of understanding but continuing to push deeper, based on pure instinct and management principles. This is a difficult area in which to provide examples but one where a senior private sector manager would probably be more skilled than others, as he/she is used to managing their own diverse organisation using these very skills.

The governors' survival kit

How then can the new governor quickly become effective in this different world where acronyms mean more than anything else and where the number of hours in the day is as always limited? I would offer the following suggestions to the new governor.

Institute a series of governors' briefings prior to each general board meeting. Governors should pick the topics and for each presentation, a particular governor should provide a brief on what exactly the presentation should cover. Alternatively a 'governor in residence' programme can often provide more useful information. In this programme each governor spends an entire day at the college, probably focusing on a particular faculty or department, getting to know that department and having an opportunity to meet staff and students and to talk through specific issues.

Members of committees should make the committee work come alive. It should not be boring and routine. Committees should take an active approach, if necessary calling people who are not on the committee to provide background information, visiting particular departments where there may be a particular issue and generally becoming a working, living part of the college rather than one of these small groups that meets late at night in the back conference room.

Where possible governors should attend external education conferences. This need not be a major time commitment but careful choice and visiting one or two of these a year can add tremendous breadth to the experience of the governor *vis a vis* his/her own institution. The governor can establish contacts with other managers, possibly other governors and in a very short period of time can get a sense of where the institution's problems fit in with those of other colleges – frequently they are similar.

This leads to the final point, that of building contacts with other colleges. This has not been easy in the polytechnic sector due to the small number of institutions but it should be substantially easier in further education. Governors can benefit from meeting their opposite numbers in other institutions. Clearly there are potential competitive boundary issues but once these are understood the benefits are considerable and area meetings of governors in similar situations should be encouraged by either the college or perhaps even the Further Education Funding Council. Failing this the governor may wish to take the initiative.

Background of governors

The following guidelines are offered to principals and chairs of formation committees to help them in their selection of governors to serve their newly formed corporations. This has to be seen against a background where many public sector organisations have moved into a form of incorporation involving external individuals on their board of governors – polytechnics, colleges of higher education, regional and district health authorities, trust hospitals and many other government agencies are now in this position. Principals and chairs and governing bodies must realise this and understand that over 600 colleges, each searching for independent governors, will have difficulty identifying eligible people who are not already over-committed. Also, the concentration of further education colleges in certain geographic areas could result in extreme competition for able people.

The board of governors in general must represent the future of the college. This means they may need to change as the college evolves. For example, if the college decides that its role is purely in vocational education within its own geographic region then the board should reflect this in order to maximise the assistance that can be provided to meet this objective. But on the other hand, if the vision would be to expand outside the immediate area and aim for national recognition the board of governors should contain some people who have an interest and knowledge of national matters.

All governors should have experience in managing change within their own organisations. Those who have never had this experience will not be able to understand the forces that will be unleashed within the college and therefore cannot participate effectively in the governance of the institution.

Many governors should have had experience of working with large workforces (difficulties in communications for example) and unions and providing the support needed in organisations employing large numbers of people. The diversity of further education colleges combined with their relative size requires this knowledge. Governors should clearly demonstrate that they are team players.

The board of governors should be diverse. A uniform group of people will not have the breadth of vision or even perhaps the risk taking nature necessary to drive home the changes required. To every extent possible the new board must be as diverse as is possible within the guidelines. It is also important to find people who have some passion about education. Somebody who has all the right business experience but is essentially not very interested in education, seeing it as good for his own curriculum vitae should be avoided.

Members of the board of governors should bring definable skills that are relevant to the institution and the changes taking place. Again, aiming for apparently important people who have no immediate relevance to the board will only bring problems at a later date.

The other feature, and a difficult one to assess, is that the governors should be a balanced group of individuals who can work together for the common good of the college. The chair of the board of governors should be quite brutal in selecting this group and removing from it people who do not work out. No selection process will be perfect. In addition he or she should be quite strong in changing the board as the circumstances of the college change, modifying it to meet the new demands placed on the board as a whole.

The governors must be prepared to devote time to the college. Nothing is worse than the early identification of those who put in the extra hours and those who do not. It quickly results in fragmentation of the board. Governors must be prepared to allocate a certain amount of time on a regular basis. I would even suggest that this must be agreed in writing so that those whose circumstances change can be politely removed within the confines of the Act.

The challenges

I think there are four basic issues that will occupy the minds of new governors.

Monitoring the move to incorporation

Firstly, how can they effectively monitor the shift from local council control to incorporation? There are many different issues to be managed, so how can they be sure that their college is on top of everything? This is probably an easier question to answer today than it was three years ago, given the experience of polytechnics and HE colleges who went through a similar process in 1989. They have a great deal of experience that can be tapped either by using people from higher education as governors or by requesting advice and assistance from the local higher education corporation.

Performance

This then leads into the issue that I think probably confronts most governors constantly – how well is our college doing? The amount of general statistics available is quite limited although there have been recent efforts in higher education that will result in a uniform performance indicator system. I suspect that while that will be successful it will take many years for further education to develop similar measures. In the meantime, how do you know that your college is doing well?

Communication

Governors frequently feel cut off from the college. They cannot communicate directly and communicating through the principal is often seen as support for management. In normal times this is not an issue but if significant problems develop, then the governors may wish to find a way of communicating more closely with the staff to show their position directly. In times of great emotion the governors are often seen as being the 'yes men' of the principal or a group of people out of touch with reality. I believe it is important for governors to find ways of bridging these gaps, and hope that some of the suggestions in this chapter could be of help.

Confidentiality

Depending on the composition of the board and the opinions of its members, confidentiality may or may not be an issue. Where it is an issue, it can inhibit the workings of the board. Put simply, most people from the private sector are used to working with confidential information. Many people within education find any mention of confidentiality to be an affront and suggestive of some form of hidden agenda. Each board will have to come to terms with this in their own way but within the confines of the law and constitutions of the corporations that are formed.

There is no doubt that the challenges facing education offer some of the most interesting management challenges at this present time. Being part of the successful development of education in the United Kingdom must offer one of the most rewarding experiences for an executive.

Reference

Polytechnics and Colleges Funding Council (1991) **Guide for governors. Polytechnics and colleges of higher education.** Guidance document. PCFC

Chapter 2: Accommodation strategies for the FE sector

Jeremy Wilson , MA MSc ARICS MRTPI
of Grimley J R Eve,
Property consultants

Introduction

This contribution outlines some of the principal property issues that colleges will have to face. It is based upon extensive experience of working with polytechnics and colleges within the PCFC (Polytechnics and Colleges Funding Council) sector of higher education; a group of institutions who have been incorporated since the 1st April 1989 and for whom property and accommodation have proved to be key issues.

From the 1st April 1993, further education and sixth form colleges will become incorporated. An integral part of that process will be the transfer to them of all property assets and liabilities. From that time the colleges will both control and own the accommodation they occupy. This will create a challenging extra dimension of responsibility and opportunity to the newly incorporated institutions.

This chapter addresses four main points:

- the importance of property;

- estate management and development as property activities to be carried out by all businesses;

- the concept of an accommodation strategy, as a method of linking overall organisational objectives with day-to-day property and accommodation decisions; and

- some of those key issues which colleges would be well advised to address in advance of incorporation.

The importance of property as a resource

Property is a key resource for most organisations and one which is often insufficiently catered for during business or organisational planning. It was Adam

Smith, the founding father of micro-economics, who first highlighted the importance of real property. He recognised that labour, capital and land were the traditional factors of production which, within an organisation, were co-ordinated to produce 'goods' or a 'service'. Thus, 'land' is an integral component of organisations to economists. The importance and financial significance of property to organisations and businesses as a whole has been recently highlighted in two extremely important pieces of research.

In 1989 the University of Reading published a report entitled **Managing operational property assets** (University of Reading 1989). The executive summary of the Reading research states:

> The purpose of this study was to obtain basic data and a broad picture of how operational property assets were managed by organisations with substantial property holdings, but for whom property was not their primary function.
>
> *Findings*
> More than half of the organisations claimed to have property assets worth 30 per cent or more of their total asset value. This confirmed the expectation that property was as significant an asset to most organisations as money and people. The overall picture was one of reactive rather than proactive property management. There was clear evidence that property was only seriously considered by organisations when they were under severe profit or cost constraints.
>
> *Property objectives*
> The majority of organisations did not clearly establish property objectives as part of their overall organisational objectives. In many instances the more general organisational objectives were not clearly expressed nor conveyed widely throughout the organisation. Operational objectives dominated decision-making, often without the impact on property assets having been explicitly assessed.
> (University of Reading 1989)

More recent research by the London Business School (London Business School 1991) confirmed the University of Reading's findings. It found that property represents an important asset in the balance sheet of companies; representing on average 150 per cent of net assets, 30-40 per cent of total assets, and 100 per cent of capital.

There is another important dimension in which property is important. Most organisations (if they require accommodation) carry out their business in a physical environment, not in a vacuum. This environment comprises both a location and a portfolio of property assets of different amenity, description, size, adequacy and tenure. This physical dimension is important because it will contribute, in a marketing sense, to the appearance and image that the organisation conveys to potential customers. This must be particularly appropriate to the education sector where, in an ever more competitive system, an ability to recruit students may be increasingly determined by what a college looks like.

More specifically, the importance of property as a resource has already become an integral consideration in the way in which the institutions in the HE sector have been required to conduct their businesses after their incorporation in 1989. Much of this impetus has come from the PCFC and there is every reason to believe that a not dissimilar approach may be applied by the proposed Further Education Funding Council.

Estate management and development

Within an organisation these two basic types of property activity take place. Estate management can be defined as, 'deployment and maintenance of the property assets to meet existing operational requirements'. This encompasses a range of activities which seeks to ensure that the business as it exists at present is properly supported in property and accommodation terms. In contrast, estate development can be defined as, 'changing property assets to support future operational needs' which is all about matching the accommodation infrastructure base to meet the needs of a changing organisation.

In reality, both types of property activity take place at the same time. However, the proportion of estate development activity that takes place is dependent upon the pressure for change. Change can come about because of financial considerations i.e. the need to realise capital, locational issues i.e. property assets located in the wrong place, or it can be associated with growth or decline of businesses and consequential changes in accommodation requirements. These different forces for change are often inter-related. In the case of the institutions in the education sector, they can best be expressed as a requirement to establish the following:

– whether the academic business is in the right place or whether existing sites can be better grouped;

– whether, from a financial point of view, asset disposals and acquisitions will be necessary;

– whether the accommodation in terms of amount, type and specification, is sufficient to accommodate the forecast growth in student numbers.

It is worth noting that the emphasis within many institutions in the PCFC sector has been upon estate development activities to support the needs of rapidly changing and growing businesses.

The principal property activities that are likely to be required include the following.

Property audit

A property database and terrier of assets is absolutely invaluable in order to know exactly what is owned.

Tenure

It is essential to establish and be quite clear as to the basis upon which these assets are actually owned. Are they freehold or leasehold? Do restrictive covenants or easements exist which might prevent the construction of new buildings, or the disposal of any assets for other than educational purposes?

Building maintenance

It should be a top priority to deal with necessary urgent building repairs. This has formed a cornerstone of activity in the PCFC sector. Key activities here will be a building condition survey coupled with a planned maintenance exercise and production of a maintenance investment plan.

Fitness for purpose

Are the buildings suitable, not just in physical terms, but also in terms of their functional requirements? Do existing rooms or spaces meet existing and projected requirements in terms of classroom size?

Value of the assets

Assets will probably have to be valued for incorporation in the balance sheet. Some form of reinstatement valuation for fire insurance purposes will be required, and particularly important there should be some estimate, for business planning purposes, of what the alternative value of the assets might be in terms of opportunity costs. For example, would it be sensible to continue operating a marginal part of the overall educational business, on a site which, if it could be released, could generate substantial value to be ploughed back into the core business on core sites?

Statutory constraints

Property activities will be constrained by the town and country planning legislation, environmental health legislation and the requirements of the fire officer. For example, there is an ever-more restrictive planning régime in operation and, once incorporated, as the PCFC sector institutions found, they could no longer benefit from the deemed planning permissions which local authorities could grant themselves for educational buildings – planning permission will have to be applied for like any other organisation or individual.

Acquisition and disposal

Colleges may well find it necessary to adopt a property strategy which requires that new accommodation be acquired or existing land and accommodation sold, or indeed, both. Therefore, before taking any action it is absolutely essential that property market issues (notably prevailing levels of value for alternative uses) are fully researched and inform the tactical approach to be taken. For example, there is no point in basing a strategy upon unrealistic assumptions as to land values or planning permissions which might be granted if assets are to be sold.

Procurement of new accommodation

Where there is a definite need for additional space then colleges will have to take some basic decisions on the nature of the project; whether to rent or buy existing space or, alternatively, to construct new space. In the latter case, what is the best means of providing the new space having regard to the variety of contractual options that exist?

The accommodation strategy

Many text books have been written about each of the main property activities outlined above and colleges will need to become conversant and advised on each of these issues when they assume responsibility for their assets. However, a fundamental point to convey is that colleges should be aware that property activities do take place within a context set by the college and this context is determined by overall organisational and educational objectives.

Consequently, there must be a business planning framework which links these overall objectives to specific property activities and initiatives. This is best achieved by the preparation of a property or accommodation strategy, which should be regarded as an important planning tool, interlinked to other college plans (notably the financial plans) and capable of being reviewed and rolled forward on a regular basis. It is certainly a concept which plays an important part for PCFC sector institutions. As such it could well be of policy relevance to FE colleges, quite apart from its advantages for business planning purposes.

PCFC published its **Guidance on estate management** (PCFC 1990) document in May 1990. This contains a specific definition of an accommodation strategy.

> An accommodation strategy is a plan for the management and development of the estate which enables the institution to deliver its academic objectives

cost effectively. It relates to the section of the institution's strategic plan concerning physical resources.

The strategy should assess existing land and buildings against the strategic goals of the institutions, evaluate opportunities and options for rationalisation and development, and set out a framework of priorities and timescales.

In view of the value and costs of land and buildings, and the lead time usually required to bring about developments of them, an accommodation strategy is essential to the sound management of institutions. It should be derived from the strategic long-term objectives of the institution.
(**Guidance on estate management**, PCFC 1990)

In brief, the accommodation strategy process is one of matching the existing property assets against the future accommodation requirements in a way which fully supports the overall corporate objectives of the organisation. The following are the key characteristics and requirements of the process.

- There has to be a clear statement of the objectives of the organisation. Otherwise, it will be difficult to assess whether or not the process of matching property assets against future accommodation requirements takes place in a way which is supportive of those objectives.

- There must be full information available on the type, amount and specification of existing accommodation.

- Future requirements (under a series of categories) must be clearly specified, primarily on a quantitative basis.

- The process should involve the generation and evaluation of options to produce a strategy which is the right one for the particular organisation.

- An accommodation strategy is a top-level exercise which will provide the context for subsequent detailing. It can only define a general or strategic direction in terms of property and accommodation requirements.

- It is important to distinguish between preparation of the strategy, on the one hand, and its implementation on the other. Providing the right information is available, an initial strategy can be prepared within a short period. What will take much longer is implementation – putting it into place; this follows on from the strategy exercise proper.

Figure 1 sets out a much simplified version of a six stage approach for the production of an accommodation strategy. It has been used in a substantial number of polytechnics and colleges and forms a sound basis for FE colleges. Clearly, each individual strategy exercise will need, in methodological terms, to be finely tuned into the particular circumstances of each college. The six stages divide neatly into two phases.

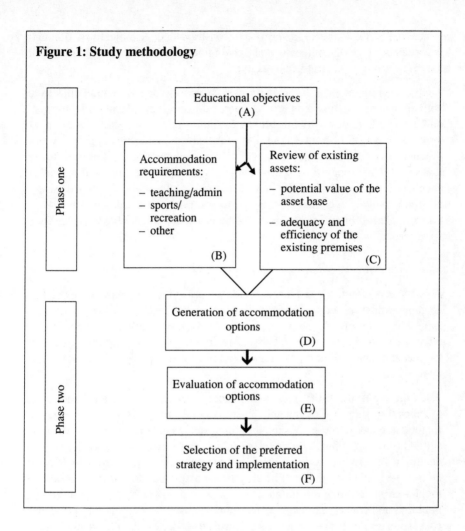

Figure 1: Study methodology

Phase one

- Educational objectives (A)
- Accommodation requirements:
  - teaching/admin
  - sports/recreation
  - other (B)
- Review of existing assets:
  - potential value of the asset base
  - adequacy and efficiency of the existing premises (C)

Phase two

- Generation of accommodation options (D)
- Evaluation of accommodation options (E)
- Selection of the preferred strategy and implementation (F)

Phase 1 is the property audit stage. This concentrates on the 'building blocks' of the accommodation strategy exercise – the assembly and analysis of basic information about existing property and accommodation assets.

Phase 2 focuses upon the generation, evaluation and selection of an accommodation strategy option, based upon the information collected in Phase 1.

Stage A: educational objectives

This stage requires an understanding of the particular objectives of the organisation and its associated accommodation and locational implications. An accommodation strategy must reflect the physical implications of these objectives. Accommodation issues should not, in theory, determine or constrain strategic objectives, although in certain instances the outcome of an accommodation strategy exercise may well have implications for strategic objectives.

Timescale is an important issue in trying to sensibly match the overall objectives with an accommodation strategy. A strategic plan in the education sector may only be able to realistically project student numbers over the short- to medium-term (say three years) yet because of the inherent characteristics of property as a product, it is very difficult to try and plan accommodation within the shorter timescale. Unlike motor cars, for example, the supply of property as a product cannot be easily switched off. Property is 'lumpy' in nature quite lengthy timescales are often involved in getting planning permission and constructing new buildings for example.Rigidities are also imposed by any requirement to lease space for a fixed term of years.

Stage B: review of existing assets

This stage is effectively a property audit of the college, under a series of key headings which are set out below. It is essential that information is available in a form which is useful for strategy purposes. Much of it will also be needed for effective estate management and, therefore, in setting up any property systems, at the outset colleges should have regard to the dual requirements of strategy and management.

The functional suitability of the assets should be assessed to establish the extent to which they support the academic objectives of the organisation, i.e. are they fit for their intended purpose? Various coding systems can be used to rank functional suitability of buildings, and analysis on this basis will enable institutions to determine how fit their accommodation stock is for the purposes for which it will be needed. Allied to this will need to be an assessment of building condition looking at the existing accommodation stock in terms of outstanding repairing liabilities and annual maintenance and running costs. It is important to establish cost estimates under these headings because any accommodation strategy should assume that those buildings and sites to be retained will have money spent on them in order to bring them back into a good and serviceable condition.

A general **assessment of the potential** of the existing property assets to accommodate additional educational buildings should also be undertaken. Is there still physical scope for constructing new buildings within the existing sites or extending and enlarging those that already exist? Some estimate of residual site capacity will assist in determining any subsequent strategy for the acquisition and disposal of property assets.

The **value of the existing property assets** should be established, both on an existing and alternative use basis. The resultant figures would be fed into an investment appraisal exercise at the quantitative evaluation stage. The value of the assets on an existing use basis can be derived using conventional valuation techniques and assumptions. However, what also needs to be established, in order to generate and evaluate options is a value of each of the properties if they were to be sold in the market for alternative use. Any organisation needs to know whether it is sitting on an asset with a very substantial opportunity cost in value terms. If the value that could be released by selling an asset for an alternative use (and with no operational penalties resulting) is significantly greater than any relocation costs associated with the transfer of existing activities, then the disposal of the asset may need to be seriously considered.

It is a combination of both property market and planning issues which will determine the prospects and level of value for alternative use. The property markets are currently in recession. However, they are cyclical and will start to rise again in due course. Any far-reaching accommodation strategy may take several years to implement and, therefore, it is important to time any disposals or acquisitions carefully and to maximum financial advantage. For example, if new space has to be acquired or land bought for construction, it could be advantageous to do it now, whilst the property market is at the bottom of the cycle, but site disposals might be best effected when the property market is buoyant.

The other determinant of alternative use potential and value is planning. The town planning system in this country will be a significant determinant in putting accommodation strategies into place. It is quite clear from recent changes in planning policies over the last few years, that there are tough times ahead for those seeking permission for development particularly on sensitive sites. However, what is interesting is that there are already signs as a result of local inquiries, that the interests of national educational policy (i.e. to expand the scale of provision) is regarded as an important planning consideration.

It is also worth emphasising that it is now a requirement that every local authority produces a statutory local plan covering the whole of its district. This presents an opportunity to get strategy proposals reflected, if at all possible, in policies and proposals of these plans. Indeed, central government has made it clear in guidance that a failure to achieve policy recognition for the proposed development will make it substantially more difficult to subsequently achieve planning permission through the appeal system.

Stage C: accommodation requirements

The purpose of this stage is to work through the future floorspace requirements of the college. The major requirement of course, is the amount of floorspace needed for teaching and adminstration purposes. This involves two steps.

Firstly, establishing the target student population on a full-time equivalent (FTE) basis. There will be different ways in which the population can be forecast and, no doubt, future guidance from the new Further Education Funding Council may well lay down ground rules. A related issue is that of the appropriate forecast date to take. Many institutions in the PCFC sector have found it useful to take both a short- to medium-term forecast date of three years and then a longer date of, say, 10 years.

Secondly the student population figures are applied to appropriate floorspace standards. The issue of space norms and new standards to be applied, could very much depend upon guidance issued by the new FEFC. What is quite clear, from experience in the PCFC sector, is that the issue of space efficiency is becoming of paramount importance in assessing space needs – funding bodies are interested in the achievement of 'value for money' in terms of accommodation. Obviously, efficiency is laudable in principle but at what stage does an overzealous application lead to an unacceptable level of congestion?

There are other categories of potential and actual accommodation requirements which are worth mentioning. These comprise:

- any residential accommodation to be provided for students;
- sports and recreational facilities; and
- any space needs arising from collaborative ventures with other organisations.

Each of these is, in itself, an important issue which merits a more detailed consideration than can be set out in this chapter.

Progress review

As a result of systematically working through the first three stages in this methodology, five particular objectives should have been achieved:

- the relationship between the overall purpose of the college and its property implications should have been spelt out in a reasonably specific manner;

- basic information should have been obtained about the accommodation features of the college;

- the accommodation should have been appraised in terms of its physical and functional suitability for the on-going business;

- there should be some indication as to the value of the property asset base, including the research into property market and planning issues;

- a clear specification of future accommodation requirements should have been set out.

The three remaining stages of the approach set out to concentrate on generating and evaluating a series of accommodation options available to the college and identifying that which best meets strategic objectives and future accommodation requirements.

Stage D: generation of options

There might be only one obvious way in which a particular college's future requirements could be met. However, as a matter of good practice, it is important to demonstrate that all reasonable options have been considered and evaluated in order that decision-makers can go ahead with confidence and commit substantial resources to putting the strategy into place. Of course, it may well be the case that generation and evaluation of a wider range of options could result in the pursuit of an option which was different to that originally preferred!

Physical accommodation options can be generated in a variety of ways. However, one approach which we have used with many institutions in the PCFC sector is to establish a spectrum of options ranging from the 'do nothing' option at one extreme to the other extreme, an option which involves the disposal of all the existing assets and the relocation of the institution to a notional greenfield site. Both options represent anchors and provide the context in which other options can be generated and evaluated. These other rationalisation options will usually involve some form of site reorganisation, either by changing the number of sites occupied and/or increasing the scale of development of certain selected sites.

A substantial number of options can in theory be generated even for colleges with a straightforward and limited asset base. There will however, be three crucial factors in getting from a theoretical longer list of options down to a much more manageable short list. These are:

- the building costs associated with each option;
- the site capacity of each option; and
- the level of capital receipt generated from disposal of surplus assets.

Stage E: evaluation of accommodation options

Evaluation should be a process which uses both quantitative and qualitative techniques. Invariably, in the evaluation process, the best option on a quantitative basis is not often going to be the best option having regard to qualitative or academic objectives and priorities. What that means, is that the best option is that which represents the best balance between the two types of evaluation. It is essential however, since they are complementary, that they are both carried out.

One useful way of carrying out **quantitative evaluation** is to use an investment appraisal approach (favoured by the PCFC) which is based upon the assumption that every option (even 'do nothing') constitutes an investment project and thus possesses its own profile of costs and benefits through a defined project period. The objective is to calculate the net present value of each option for comparative purposes.

One of the most problematic issues is how to undertake effective **qualitative evaluation**. The qualitative criteria for the assessment of options should be those which represent the issues and requirements of most importance to the college – thus the significance of properly expressing the relationship between the overall organisation objectives of the college and, possible accommodation requirements at Stage A. Difficulties can arise because non-quantitative techniques are being applied to assess each option. For example, if there are a dozen criteria for qualitative assessment, can they all be accorded the same weight? If not, how does one measure their differential importance? It is easy to see how quickly those evaluating options on a qualitative basis can be sucked into some form of spurious cost-benefit analysis.

Stage F: selection and implementation of the preferred option

As a result of Stages D and E a preferred option will emerge. The purpose of Stage F is to specify precisely what the option consists of and to provide the link between the general strategy and its implementation. In doing so, the following key points need to be considered:

- there should be a clear statement of the strategy in terms of the content, time-scale and funding;

- the strategy should be demonstrably robust and capable of being implemented, or at least not deflected off course by subsequent events;

- the areas where the strategy might be vulnerable should be identified and appropriate measures or 'fall-back' positions identified;

- the strategy should specify what further tasks need to be carried out to firm up the strategy and give it more substance. It is inherent in a strategy exercise of this type that the recommended option cannot be specified in great detail and indeed, to do so would often be premature.

- the strategy, together with further refinement and detailing tasks, should then be set out in some form of a key activity programme or critical path, to enable decision-makers to identify what needs to be done at what stage and in what sequence.

- it is also important in ensuring effective implementation of a strategy, to identify the different types of audiences or decision-makers, to whom an accommodation strategy will have to be presented, and with whom negotiations will have to take place. Implementation should also address the different ways in which these audiences inter-relate with each other and the best way in which to secure support and commitment from all concerned;

- finally, implementation calls for a very strong project management approach. If strategies are to be pursued effectively, the college should organise its resources in a purposeful fashion. There will be a need for strong control, co-ordination and commitment.

Conclusions and next steps

The first, and basic, message which I hope has been conveyed in this chapter is the importance of property as a resource to the organisation as a whole. Property has a specific and important part to play within the total organisational planning process, a factor which is now well appreciated by most institutions in the higher education sectors. This, in turn, creates a requirement for a business-like approach towards estate management and development activities. Whilst many of these will need to be carried out as a matter of course, they will benefit from the provision of a property context in order to prioritise and determine the thrust of effort. In this chapter I have set out an approach which proposes that an accommodation strategy is an appropriate way of providing the property brief for an institution, which brings with it the following specific benefits:

- a structured approach, following a recognisable sequence of activities, should lead towards the right conclusion and correct strategy. This must be preferable to a property brief which is really just a wish list of accommodation aspirations with little in the way of substantiation or evidence to justify it;

- if the correct context at the strategic level is established, then the right decisions on property and accommodation can be made;

- prioritisation means that effort will be expended and finance directed towards the projects and activities that are critical or fundamental to the achievement of the strategy. Money is always a scarce resource and should always be directed to where it is most needed;

- a logical approach to producing a property context (i.e. an accommodation strategy) means that a reasonable programme with attached timescales, or a critical path, can be established to guide the institutions towards successful implementation.

Despite the fact that incorporation is still some way off, it is quite clear, if the PCFC sector experience is anything to go by, that it is those institutions who 'hit the ground running' that are more likely to be successful in addressing and putting into place growth and rationalisation strategies at an early stage. This will inevitably mean that the following key issues will have to be addressed prior to incorporation.

- In setting up any new organisational structure for the post-incorporation college what importance is to be placed on property, as a resource, and what mechanisms will be put in place for decision-making?

- Whilst the definition of assets and liabilities under the Act will effectively be a matter of legal interpretation, and not policy preference, there will probably be scope for many colleges to reach agreement with their respective local education authorities which enable policy issues to prevail. This means that, in the short-term, colleges will at least need to ensure that they do not agree to give up assets or agree to enter into arrangements which could subsequently prejudice future property strategies. This issue may raise an associated requirement to make representations on emerging policies and proposals in district-wide plans.

- At a technical level, colleges should consider their property database requirements which, if properly thought out, can make material contributions to the overall organisational planning process, in matters such as space utilisation, the recording and apportionment of running cost information and providing information required for decision-making on policy issues.

- Who is going to be responsible for resourcing the property function? Colleges will need to consider a range of issues where expertise is required; the extent to which that expertise is a continuing or a one-off requirement; and the depth of expertise needed in each case. Resolutions to these issues will determine, for example, the extent to which property activities will need to be resourced in-house or combined with either, or both, selective and recurrent expertise from external property consultants. Every college's requirement will differ but it is important to ensure that the right type and level of expertise is available in each case.

References

London Business School (1991) **The place of commercial property in the UK economy.** London Business School

Polytechnics and Colleges Funding Council (1990) **Guidance on estate management.** PCFC

University of Reading (1989) **Managing operational property assets.** University of Reading

Chapter 3: Estate management in the PCFC sector

John Avery
Head of Estate Management
Higher Education Funding Council (England)

PCFC and FEFC

I should preface this chapter by a health warning, or disclaimer. I am going to refer to the way things work in the PCFC (Polytechnics and Colleges Funding Council) sector. This is not necessarily how it will be in the FE sector but it may be reasonable to assume that successful PCFC policies and methods might influence the development of the FE sector. That remains to be seen. I am not speaking for the FE Funding Council but hope to give you some insight about the way one government agency interacts with its funded institutions in similar circumstances to those that may be found in the FE sector.

Independence

In April 1989 each of the 83 polytechnics and colleges who were not already independent became an independent concern with a board responsible for the financial health of the organisation. They own property and other assets which are used to deliver their products and are in competition with other businesses for the customers in a growth market.

This financial independence means that those that could once have sought financial support from their local education authority if their books did not balance, or if some catastrophe occurred to their buildings, now stand alone. They wish to grow, to expand their buildings and to improve their facilities. Independence means that their assets are now private property and they raise funds in many new ways, including grants from industry and commerce, loans secured on property, sale and leaseback and business expansion schemes. This new flexibility enables them to create reserves, to budget and to provide from their own resources new student accommodation, teaching blocks, libraries and lecture theatres and to upgrade existing assets to meet the requirements of educational needs as the turn of the century approaches.

Government and the PCFC

The Minister for Higher Education confirmed in a speech in November 1990,

'The Government's role in higher education is not to plan or direct the system in detail, it is to develop a framework within which institutions and their various clients can interact efficiently ... the general thrust of government policy is towards developing a more market-orientated framework for the future development of our higher education system. Strength is derived not from monolithic centralism but from the autonomy of individual institutions.'

Challenges

So, while the Government and the PCFC respectively seek to increase the supply of applicants for student places and assist in funding those places, the responsibility for providing for 400,000 higher education students currently, and some 800,000 by the year 2015, lies with the 83 autonomous polytechnics and colleges.

In addition to having to find a way of accepting double the present numbers of students in the next 25 years, they face a number of challenges, none of which is easy, partly because many institutions have had little experience of estate management in its widest sense. First, they inherited estates which were in poor condition and which needed a considerable amount of money, and dedicated attention to set them to rights. Second, the accommodation which they have is unequal – some have too much, others insufficient. Third, much of the estate is out-of-date for the purposes of modern teaching methods. As autonomous institutions they now manage their estates in such a way that they can solve many of these problems largely from their own resources.

Condition of the buildings

The PCFC was from the beginning aware of the poor conditions in part of the sector and, to identify the scale of the problem and to assist in making a case to the Government for funds, commissioned a survey of buildings in the sector (PCFC 1989). The report by the surveyors showed the need for £626m over five years, of which £75m was needed to be spent within one year to deal with urgent problems affecting health and safety and a further £188m within two years to deal with other urgent structural problems. It was more than the individual institutions could be expected to handle and the Government did provide PCFC with some £160m over three years to help with the most urgent work. It is expected that the adoption of pro-active estate management policies will lead to rationalisation and the avoidance of some of the work, but institutions will still have the responsibility of supplementing the grant in order to make good their property, and to have a sound maintenance investment plan to ensure the proper upkeep of their property. This will enable them to budget properly, avoid wasteful expenditure on buildings which it is intended to dispose of and form the basis of a suitable planned maintenance programme.

Options

Institutions have, among the opportunities available to them, one or more of the following:

- improve the efficiency with which they use existing property;

- expand capacity by using the buildings for more of the time available;

- dispose of surplus property and reapply the proceeds to new buildings;

- dispose of inefficient property and replace it with better;

- borrow on the security of existing property to build further accommodation;

- acquire further accommodation by leasing;

- expand capacity by franchising to other educational establishments with excess space;

- apply to the PCFC for capital grant for new buildings.

One of the most important features of the transition from public to autonomous status is that all the other options are considered before adopting the final solution above. There is a change of emphasis. Instead of being the first, and often only, source of funds for property investment, public funds (previously from the LEAs and DES, now the PCFC) are the last. Colleges and polytechnics now look first at their own resources in order to solve their problems and achieve their ambitions.

Efficient use of property

Polytechnics and colleges requiring new buildings originally referred to the DES Design Notes for guidance on the space requirements for particular kinds of accommodation and for students in specified courses. The PCFC adopted the standards but tightened up the method of measurement. This had the effect of making the space standards a bit tighter. Many institutions, particularly the larger ones, are able to operate with less space than the norms would suggest is needed, typically 70 per cent. Although it is acknowledged that some of the smaller institutions, typically some of the very specialised ones, find it difficult to achieve efficiencies as good as this, the PCFC does give particular weight in allocating capital to space efficiency. In other words, it is assumed that only colleges which are well below the norms need capital expenditure to enable them to absorb growth.

Naturally it is not really that simple. Some of the problems that colleges have to deal with are associated with out-moded accommodation or buildings which are incapable of being used efficiently. It is quite a blunt instrument.

Traditionally, the education year is about 38 weeks, each of five days, and each day is eight hours, except for Wednesday, which ends at lunchtime for games, Monday which starts later, and Friday which finishes earlier. Several polytechnics have developed the considerable potential for more intensive use of the premises by extending the hours of use in the day (some polytechnics already work a 12-hour day) and possibly the number of days in the week and even the weeks in the year (perhaps by a four-term arrangement).

Many institutions have found that new timetabling methods can improve the utilisation of existing teaching areas and relieve the pressure for further accommodation.

By these, and other means, institutions have found that they can accommodate many more students in buildings once thought to have reached capacity.

Rationalisation

The buildings which the institutions inherited on independence were a mixed collection. They included precious parts of the architectural heritage as well as the more unfortunate manifestations of concrete mass building; some provided high standards of comfort and environment, others suffered health hazards and squalor.

Those institutions with well-maintained property in pleasant surroundings are well placed to generate income by quickly developing their potential in the competitive world of short courses and conferences. Those not so fortunate have inherited a backlog of repairs costing millions of pounds.

A few have valuable surplus assets which they can realise to self-fund improvements in accommodation; others (usually away from the southeast) have assets whose value falls well short of the amounts needed for new buildings or major restoration.

Strategy

Each institution prepares a business plan (its strategic plan) which identifies its objectives. It covers things like the range of courses which it proposes to offer, the number of students that it plans to recruit, its staffing, any mergers which it intends to pursue and all matters relevant to the management of an educational organisation over a period of time. Part of the plan covers 'physical resources', the capital base of the polytechnic or college. This section is expressed in very general terms; the subject is covered in detail in the separate 'accommodation strategy'.

Accommodation strategy

Traditionally the polytechnics obtained much of their property by a system owing more to accident than planning. In a climate of expanding demand for student places and pressure for more accommodation, but little money for it, the local education authorities added to their higher educational buildings whatever became available – redundant schools, warehouses and the ubiquitous mobile premises. College premises were part of the authorities' overall estates and rarely was there an ethos of a structured approach to estate management at an institutional level.

Now the emphasis has changed. Estate management is no longer limited to maintenance, minor improvements and attempting to gain extensions and new buildings; institutions now have to make their assets work for them and that means adopting a pro-active approach to managing the asset with the greatest potential – property. One of the largest polytechnics, Sheffield, is embarking on phase one of a rationalisation programme, which will eventually result in not only a facelift and expansion of its central city Pond Street site, but the disposal of its three other sites and development of a completely new site.

In the past, estate management was reactive. Colleges were allocated buildings which were surplus to other requirements – an old school, for example – or expansion was accommodated by taking a lease of the most suitable building that happened to be available. Property transactions were largely opportunistic, now they are strategic – consistent with a plan, the accommodation strategy, that identifies the type of opportunity that should be taken. It is, however, not a list of items which the institution would like (although it will include that). It is a fundamental assessment of the estate, its problems and the options for solution.

The accommodation strategy covers the adequacy, suitability and condition of the existing estate, the problems to be solved, the opportunities available, the projects to be pursued, the timescale and sources of funding.

The suitability of premises, ignoring for the time being their condition, varies from the ideal down to the intolerable and the units scrutinised range from as small as a single room to as large as a complete campus. Some polytechnic sites, full of individually satisfactory teaching and learning buildings, are unsatisfactory as a whole because of their distance from the central campus. In such cases each of the sites is unsatisfactory in relation to the other, even though satisfactory in itself. The strategy often includes as one possible solution the disposal of one or the other, or both.

Using staff in the estates and building management team or expertise brought in from outside, the maintenance and repair requirements are identified and costed. This is one of the contributory factors in the accommodation strategy, but not the only one, because all the facts – suitability as well as condition and other matters still to be discussed – when stirred into the strategic porridge, determine whether a building will justify repairs or not. If it does, the building features in the maintenance investment plan as one to be maintained and to form part of the planned maintenance programme. If the strategy identifies the building as a candidate for disposal or replacement, it features in the plan as requiring enough attention to retain its value and use for the required period only.

This process identifies the problems, but the solutions vary from repair or adaptation to redevelopment or complete relocation. The objective of achieving value for money from the funds allocated to deal with the repair backlog referred to earlier requires a comparison of the costs of a replacement building with the costs of repairing the existing one. The money intended for repairs might show a better return if used as a contribution to a new building.

The problems are first prioritised and interrelated, and identified as those with only cost implications (such as disrepair) and those needing more drastic solutions (such as inherent unsuitability). There will often be a number of possible solutions to a problem – build, lease, buy, rationalise. All cost money and are compared with one another, and with taking no action, by a process of financial evaluation. This stage often requires outside expertise from surveyors, valuers, architects and planners to provide the values and assumptions used in the evaluations. There is considerable overlap with the next stage, 'Opportunities'.

Opportunities

A number of institutions have found opportunities to assist in a rationalisation process: for instance, playing fields with potential for planning permission may be sold for development value and be replaced by land at closer to agricultural value; a town centre teaching building sold for office development may produce enough to make a major contribution to its replacement with a more suitable building at a more appropriate location.

After the above evaluation has been carried out, the institution determines which projects it wishes to pursue, how and when it is going to fund them and, maybe, how much grant it may need to assist it.

PCFC capital

In addition to its revenue grant, the PCFC is put in possession of capital funds by the Secretary of State to invest in development in higher education and, as previously mentioned, to assist institutions with the problems of their backlog of maintenance.

Capital funds are intended for a variety of defined purposes. These include equipment and minor building works, but can include specific funds for major building or other investment projects. The total amount for capital for the next three years is over £130m per annum, of which £70m in the first year has been allocated for equipment and £67m for buildings-related expenditure. Of this £45m is needed for backlog repairs and minor works and £17m for committed projects, leaving only £5m which can be used to start new projects. For 1992/93 the demand totalled £70m.

Private finance

Although polytechnics and colleges were used in pre-incorporation days to getting the whole of their capital projects funded by their local authority, or central government, the PCFC now funds on average half the cost of a project; the other half having to come from reserves built up by the college, disposal of surplus assets or borrowing. It has to be said that there have been difficulties in getting financial institutions to understand the education sector to a sufficient extent to give them confidence to lend. This particularly applies when assets are required as security for the loan because a large number of the polytechnic and college buildings are encumbered by a former local authority debt charge. There may be a difference here between the inheritance of FE colleges and that enjoyed by the polytechnics. The polytechnics inherited all debt, however old, and this distinction may prove a difficult obstacle to the raising of private finance.

Unfortunately, college assets are not in any event considered with great favour by lending institutions. The bottom line for them, of course, is whether they could sell the asset if the college defaulted on its repayments, and who wants to buy the average college? If there is a market value, a lending institution is going to be loath to close down a building, remove the staff and students and sell it.

This means that the main security that lending institutions are looking for is the ability of the college to service and repay the debt out of its income and their judgement on this depends very much upon their confidence in the sector as a whole and the institution concerned in particular. Lending institutions try to get the PCFC to act as a safety net, effectively to underwrite the responsibilities of the college but, not surprisingly, it is not prepared to.

Polytechnics suffer from the problem that they have not been independent for very long and consequently cannot show lending institutions a track record of effective management. Banks therefore rely largely upon their judgement of an institution by forming views about its management expertise (particularly financial management). They seem to take a certain amount of comfort from the rigorous monitoring procedures of the PCFC which are designed to ensure that institutions do retain financial viability.

Despite the best endeavours of institutions to generate development, maximise efficiency in the intensity of use of their buildings, and raise private finance the sector will still need government capital for projects which are essential to enable the growth in demand to be met. The PCFC has to ensure that whatever it does produces the best value for money, not only with each institution but in the sector as a whole.

Accountability

Higher education institutions, while publicly funded, are not themselves in the public sector. They own the legal title to their property but, because they receive public funds and because much of their property was publicly funded (either directly by the DES or through local authorities), they agree, in a contract with the PCFC (the financial memorandum) to certain restrictions on their freedom to use those funds and assets. The PCFC bids for funds from the Secretary of State as part of the annual Public Expenditure Survey; it allocated to its institutions in 1990-91 just over £1bn, identified as revenue and capital. While it is mindful of the charge from the Secretary of State that its arrangements should not be excessively bureaucratic; as the spender of over £1bn of public money each year the PCFC has to assure itself that the money is spent most effectively. The conditions imposed by the financial memorandum relate to matters such as the management of the institution, its accounting procedures, its duty to provide information; and the circumstances in which the PCFC consent to certain activities is required. Just as the PCFC is responsible to Parliament for the use it makes of its funds, so it is responsible for the use made in the sector of assets which were originally publicly funded. It is in this last area that the PCFC and the institutions relate most closely in maximising the potential in the sector for growth of the building capacity.

Under the terms of the financial memorandum each institution undertakes to:

- secure the efficient, economical and effective management of all the institution's resources and expenditure, including funds other than those provided by the Council, capital assets and equipment, and manpower, so that the investment of public funds in the institution by the Council is not placed at risk;

- keep its land holdings under review with the objective of rationalising and disposing of those which are no longer needed;

- obtain PCFC consent to borrowing above specified limits or to use local authority funded assets as security;

- obtain PCFC consent to land transactions involving public funds.

Before giving any consent which is required under the terms of the financial memorandum, or considering any capital grant, the PCFC needs to have evidence of soundly-based estate management.

Investment appraisal

Each investment or property transaction involving funding (revenue or capital) from the PCFC or publicly funded assets has to satisfy the requirement that, of all the courses that institution could adopt, the proposed project offers the best value for money and, if PCFC capital is required, it has furthermore to satisfy the PCFC that it gives better value for money than other competing claims for those funds. The PCFC in funding investment projects has to impose selection criteria to ensure maximum value for money, the most economic investment and the most effective use of its funds. The criteria are:

(1) that the institution has an accommodation strategy and maintenance investment plan consistent with its strategic plan; and

(2) that the project is consistent with these plans and, using investment appraisal techniques, it has been compared with all other reasonable options for solving the problem and represents the best value for money.

Human resources

It may by now be obvious that there are many levels of activity and skills required in managing and developing college estates; from maintaining the boilers and making sure the doors are secure to evaluating the alternative uses of town centre sites and formulating financial strategy. The shift in emphasis in the PCFC from a project driven approach to a strategic one has lifted the profile of estate management in the colleges so that the key participants in property decisions are the directors. This is not to say that building and estate managers are not required, they are; but it is very difficult for someone who is usually up to his eyes in the day-to-day problems of keeping the services running, organising routine maintenance, designing and arranging adaptations and the thousand other things that a buildings manager has to do: it is difficult for him to change the scale of his thinking. The roof is leaking – is there any money in the budget to pay for it? Is it more important than the broken flagstones outside the Students' Union or the falling mosaic over the director's window? How much will it cost? Get quotations and see if it can be done. The first question should have been – should the roof be mended? Should we be in that building at all?

In the polytechnics and colleges the tension between these two opposing demands has been resolved by devolving strategic responsibility to a deputy director whose responsibilities often include finance as well.

Conclusion

I hope this has given a flavour of the property activity in the PCFC sector and the way in which the Council hopefully helps institutions to develop and become more effective alongside its obligations to Parliament for the use of public funds. Don't be frightened of it; independence is exciting and challenging and full of opportunities. The worst thing is a closed mind.

Reference

Polytechnics and Colleges Funding Council (1989) **Building condition survey of polytechnics and colleges.** PCFC

Chapter 4: Personnel policy

John Skitt
Principal
Barnet College

This chapter is concerned with personnel policy. It examines the purpose of a personnel policy, considers its scope, makes some suggestions about the implementation of aspects of the policy and explores some of the central issues in making the policy effective.

Purpose of a personnel policy

Many colleges are large and virtually all are complex organisations employing a wide range of staff on very different conditions of employment. It is intriguing to think that most colleges have operated in the past without a personnel policy and the stimulus to develop one arises from the prospect of fulfilling employer responsibilities in the near future. A primary purpose of the policy is to enable employer responsibilities to be carried out in an explicit and systematic way. It is vital that all staff have one document, freely available, to which they can turn, which sets out the college's position and arrangements for all the matters that directly affect staff. The personnel policy must fulfil at least this basic function. Ideally it should be much more than that. Staff account for between 70 and 80 per cent of the college revenue budget. The quality of our students' learning, the extent to which their experience at college enriches their lives and achieves new thresholds for future development, is heavily dependent upon the staff. The personnel policy should focus on the arrangements to effectively select, support, train and develop staff in response to changing student, organisational and industrial needs. It should provide for organisational review and adjustment and for management development and acquisition of demanding new skills and strategies.

Staff are also at the heart of all finance, academic and premises issues. They are the single most influential and most time consuming of our resources: decisions about the budget are often to do with staffing and the use of staff time. 'People–power planning' needs to be a central concern, as does our use of our accommodation and equipment. The personnel policy, therefore, is not only essential to the implementation of the development, corporate and business plans, it should also inform and influence their formulation.

Scope of the personnel policy

The personnel policy should set out the arrangements for the following:

- staff planning and review of posts;
- job information;
- recruitment and selection procedures;
- staff development and induction;
- review and appraisal;
- professional advice for individuals;
- industrial relations and health and safety;
- placing people issues at the centre.

Staff planning and review of posts

Staff planning should enable us to better meet our existing needs and to predict and then meet our future needs more effectively. Those within the organisation will be best placed to make these judgements based on thorough organisational analysis of:

- patterns of work;
- categories of employment;
- age profiles;
- gender and ethnic breakdown;
- disability;
- grades and length of service;
- qualifications and experience;
- staff development and training required or received;
- career/personal aspirations;

in conjunction with local and regional influencing factors such as:

- industrial trends;
- employment patterns, skills surpluses and shortages;
- rates of pay in competing jobs;
- housing/transportation factors.

These analyses should be updatable either on demand or at known times, such as annual cycles of budget preparation, review of development plan and key recruitment periods.

The review of posts will be more effective when the above information is readily available. The regular review, and if necessary, the redistribution of posts when vacancies arise, will ensure a match between college needs and policy objectives and the staff establishment and its deployment. The review of posts should initially take place as close as possible to the point of delivery. The course or subject team, or group of staff delivering a review, should make recommendations to those managing their programme or course area, department, faculty etc. The senior management team should approve recommendations and take final decisions or pass them to the principal or governing body as appropriate. It is, however, critical that staffing decisions are taken corporately, are based on thorough analysis and the reasons are explicitly known.

The process of review and consultation will take account of local and national agreements, institutional or development plans, available resources, staffing structure and all posts, job descriptions and personnel specifications.

Job information

Each post should have a clear job description which sets out the main duties, to whom they are responsible, and for whom they are responsible. (**Figure 2** sets out the information to be considered in formulating a job description.) As people's duties change over time, each post should be reviewed on an annual basis. Many colleges will have job profiles for all teaching staff arising from the 1987-89 national agreement and job descriptions for recently advertised posts. This information should provide a useful basis for drawing up job descriptions in consultation with postholders and the teams in which they work.

The personnel policy should set out the arrangements for the initial set of job descriptions and then ensure procedures when vacancies occur or new posts are required. It is important that the procedures are known and that they are followed. A clear picture of the purpose of each post and its connections and relationships with other posts is a vital ingredient in ensuring that the requirements of the area and the organisation are met.

In the case of vacancies or new posts, the job description should be used to draw up a personnel specification. The personnel specification will set out the organisation's view of the personal qualities, skills, knowledge, experience and qualifications which will be necessary for the person appointed to carry out the tasks required by the post. It should also assist in determining the post's suitability for the applicant.

Figure 2: Information which should be included in the job description.

- Post title and number – this will relate to the college establishment
- Salary scale
- Location of the job
- Main purpose of the post
- Main duties of the post
- Other responsibilities
- To whom responsible
- With whom the appointee will work
- Responsibilities for other staff
- Financial responsibilities
- Responsibilities for equipment, stock
- Teaching commitment
- Physical conditions
- Career prospects
- Prospects for staff development
- Any other relevant details

(extracted from Barnet College personnel policy)

Recruitment and selection procedures

One of the main areas of the college's activity in the past to excite confusion, derision and sometimes resentment has been the recruitment and selection procedures. The personnel policy should set out clearly the organisation's arrangements in these areas.

With staff planning and job information mechanisms firmly in place, procedures for recruitment should become more straightforward, predictable and efficient. The college can set out its processes for recruitment and expect them to be followed. **Figure 3** gives a summary of the recruitment process contained in Barnet College's personnel policy.

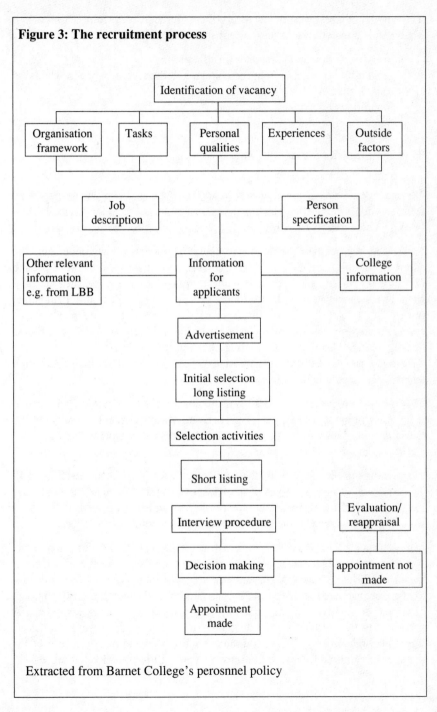

Figure 3: The recruitment process

Identification of vacancy

- Organisation framework
- Tasks
- Personal qualities
- Experiences
- Outside factors

Job description — Person specification

Other relevant information e.g. from LBB — Information for applicants — College information

Advertisement

Initial selection long listing

Selection activities

Short listing

Interview procedure

Decision making — appointment not made — Evaluation/ reappraisal

Appointment made

Extracted from Barnet College's perosnnel policy

51

It is important that each candidate receives a comprehensive picture of the college when requesting details of a post. These should include:

- job description and personnel specification;
- general information about the college and the area of work in which the post is placed;
- conditions of service;
- equal opportunities policies;
- summary of other college policies;
- timescale for the recruitment procedures;
- conditions of appointment.

The line manager, in consultation with the appropriate department and the personnel team, should formulate the selection timetable and set out the selection methods to be used. The duration and variety of the process will differ between jobs.

The selection procedure should ensure that all applicants clearly understand the nature of the job for which they are applying, appreciate the context of the job including support for college policies, and meet potential colleagues. The procedure should be seen as valid and fair, with the principle of confidentiality maintained throughout to safeguard the interests of the candidates. The principle of confidentiality need not work against an open and participative selection process as long as candidates in making an application are made clearly aware of the recruitment process. For example, that relevant colleagues will see their application and will participate in the selection process.

The selection process should seek to ensure that the person most well equipped to undertake the job is offered the post. There are always elements of subjectivity. Our aim should therefore be to reduce these subjective elements and hence the possibility of a mismatch between person and post.

The selection process starts with the arrangements for recruitment (see **Figure 4**). The arrangements for all stages of the selection process – from initial longlisting to the design of the programmes for candidates and the link with induction – should be put in place by the time the post is advertised.

In most instances it is advisable to have at the least a two-stage selection programme. The first or preliminary stage should enable the candidate to learn as much about the job and the college as possible, and for college staff to learn about the candidates. This element should include exercises, case studies and simulations. Students can of course be involved in the process – and perhaps more often should be. A presentation by candidates for a lecturer's post to a group of students has its limitations but also its values. Candidates must be made clearly aware of the preparation required for any activities which are part of the selection process.

Figure 4: Elements of the selection process

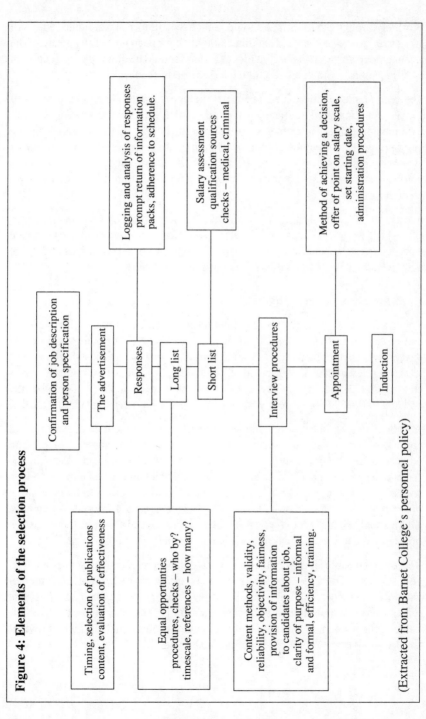

(Extracted from Barnet College's personnel policy)

53

Working through the first stage should reduce the number of candidates who will go forward to the next stage. Candidates should have been made fully aware of the arrangements for short-listing – a process which should be thorough and recorded, as unsuccessful candidates should have the right to feedback.

The second stage will be a more formal dialogue or interview, with a panel or panels including the line manager and other staff who will be working closely with the appointee. The personnel officer should be invited to join panels where appropriate. There may be occasions when it is not essential for the principal or vice-principal to sit on a panel. It is, however, important that one of them is involved at some stage, primarily to ensure that the route follows laid down procedures.

It is inevitable that thorough and systematic selection procedures will on occasions take a little longer. It may seem costly to invest time – say two days – to complete a process, but the benefits in terms of more appropriate appointments and in the perceived fairness of the process are worth the extra costs.

Staff development and induction

The quality of the selection process should be reinforced by an ongoing, relevant and comprehensive staff development process. Those colleges that still do not have a staff development policy should formulate one. The policy should set out the objectives of staff development and include purposes for individuals, teams and the organisation and demonstrate clearly the values and expectations of the college. Barnet College's policy, shown in Figure 4, has been in place since 1982.

A cornerstone of the staff development process is the induction programme. All colleagues whether as individuals or in groups, regardless of starting time, should participate in the programme to introduce, inform and welcome them to the college. It is the bridge between appointment and being integrated into the college community. The process should consist of an initial induction and a continuing programme. Both should provide for college-wide, area and workplace elements. There should be a thorough checklist of items to be addressed in the induction programme and a set of materials available to support the programme.

Wherever possible all new colleagues should have a mentor who acts as a guide, counsellor and friend to them in their first six months or year in post. The mentor should be trained for the role and those participating should be chosen for the relevance of their skills and experience, and in particular because they see the value of the role. Many colleges now also have a professional tutor who provides similar support to all staff at an institutional level.

Figure 5: Barnet College staff development policy

The policy will be to:

(i) encourage job satisfaction, personal achievement, individual and team effort, and thus provide for personal advancement within the college or outside it;

(ii) develop staff in ways which will help to maintain and improve the overall effectiveness of the college in meeting the vocational, general educational and leisure needs of the community;

(iii) help colleagues to maintain and improve teaching skills and methods, particularly in the light of changing educational and personal needs;

(iv) marry, where possible, the interests and needs of the individual and the department or college;

(v) ensure that all colleagues have an opportunity for development through the operation of an explicit and systematic process.

The induction process will assist in shaping the expectations of staff development as a whole. Staff development should of course be closely linked to an annual review of professional development and performance or appraisal. The consequent training needs profiles and institutional or development plans will provide the context for the programme of training and developmental activities. One main dimension of staff development is to provide opportunities for staff to take on different challenges and tasks, work with different teams, assume new roles. Another is to provide for the development of existing skills or the acquisition of new skills and knowledge by secondment, placement or attendance on courses.

External activities are one means of meeting needs, whether by short workshops and conferences or longer courses, sometimes leading to a qualification. The in-house programme has become the focus of training in many colleges. An in-house programme enables provision to be tailored specifically to the needs of groups and the organisation, to draw on the skills and experience of both internal and external contributors, to be located within the college or externally and to be arranged on the most convenient times to the institution.

The personnel policy should identify how the in-house programme is designed and implemented, how colleagues are informed of activities and how they apply to participate or to arrange events of relevance to their own area. Colleges may decide to have staff dedicated to their in-house programme. Perhaps a staff development officer, a branch of the college development unit or a member of the personnel team. Staff will need to be clear about responsibilities of those involved with designing and implementing the staff development policy.

Some colleges may wish to collaborate with other colleges in the delivery of programmes in order to share resources and costs. The nature of arrangements and procedures should be addressed.

The evaluation of the staff development process should occur systematically at a number of levels. Any (preferably annual) review of the development plan should take account of the achievements of the process, probably drawing on evaluation by the academic board, its staff development sub-committee or the senior management team. Another level of evaluation is the annual review or appraisal itself where both manager and managed can assess the previous year's action.

In ensuring that staff have an opportunity to reach their full potential, it is difficult to over-emphasise the centrality of the staff development process for all staff.

Review and appraisal

The personnel policy should set out the arrangements for the performance review and appraisal of all staff. In particular it should make the purpose of the process clear, and its relationship (if any) to pay, conditions, discipline and grievance. There are powerful, and in my view overwhelming, arguments for explicitly separating review and appraisal from these matters.

The personnel policy cannot expect to detail the full provisions of an appraisal scheme. The scheme itself should be distributed to all staff. The personnel policy may well identify or summarise the main elements of the scheme (shown in **Figure 6**), or record them in an appendix, identify the procedure for re-negotiating or changing the scheme and emphasise to staff the importance of being familiar with the scheme. The close relationship to staff development and professional development could be highlighted.

The role and responsibilities of managers in the appraisal process should be clearly identified. Detailed analyses and experience of appraisal are available (Duckett 1990 and Barnet College 1989).

Professional advice for individuals

Staff have a host of personal issues about which they may wish to seek advice, from early retirement arrangements to compassionate leave. Their own trade union is an important and valuable source of information, and in the past good employing local authorities have provided systematic and easily accessible advice. A primary source of advice should be, and will have to be in the future, from within the college. It is good management practice to provide easily accessible, reliable and supportive guidance to colleagues on all issues concerning conditions of service, entitlements and ways of analysing or approaching sometimes complex individual circumstances.

A person's line manager can be the initial contact and will be able to resolve some matters. The line manager, however, requires the backup of the personnel team or officer. The personnel team should comprise dedicated professionals who see its advisory role as being equally available to managers and managed.

Many matters of conditions of service will require negotiation and interpretation at institutional level – we may even see college-based bargaining on pay and conditions – and a professional personnel team, preferably in-house or if necessary shared between institutions is essential.

The personnel policy should emphasise the importance of this service and indicate the range of advice which is available.

Industrial relations and health and safety

The personnel policy should set out the college's arrangements for conducting industrial relations. All participants in the activities of the college need to be fully aware of their respective duties, responsibilities and entitlements so that they can act within legal requirements and national and local conditions of service.

Staff should be conversant with the procedures for consultation and negotiation between management and unions. In colleges which seek to practice an open and democratic, participative style of management, there should be emphasis on that style and the supportive and facilitating role that managers should practice.

Matters of health and safety have often been given scant attention in further education, sometimes due to pressures on resources. That situation cannot continue. Managers will need to be very much more aware of and committed to their responsibilities under the **Health and Safety at Work Act** 1974. The employees should also be fully aware of their own individual programme areas of the college.

Placing people issues at the centre

Above all the personnel policy should seek to be 'user-friendly'. The way in which it is written, set out and produced will be as important as the content. The content should demonstrate that the organisation places a central importance on people issues and indeed provides that focus in itself. Those colleges who place a strong emphasis on the people management responsibilities of their senior managers, should ensure that that is reflected in the personnel policy – doing so will be an important step in ensuring that the policy is effective.

Making the personnel policy effective

Making the personnel policy effective will not be an easy task for many colleges. To some staff, a personnel policy will smack of industry; and perhaps be culturally difficult to accept. There are no clear-cut or easy solutions. It will be primarily a matter of building up people's confidence and gradually being able to demonstrate that the policy has value and is a support as well as a safeguard.

There are a number of matters which may, however, assist the policy and its implementation.

Involve the unions

Provide an opportunity for the unions to be involved from the outset. Discuss with them the objectives and principles of the policy, seek their views and offer an opportunity for the unions to be involved in formulating the policy. If they decline, the policy can be circulated in draft form for comment and consultation.

In addition; it is important to ensure that staff are fully informed of the development by managers.

Recruit a professional personnel team

Once formulated the policy will require constant attention if it is to be implemented effectively.

It will in itself be a source of action and follow up. The principal has an important strategic role, and senior managers should draw on the policy constantly. Nevertheless, the core activity in implementing the policy must come from the personnel team. Every college, or group of colleges, will require a team of experienced, professional personnel staff, whose central remit is personnel issues. Their credibility will be established by the way in which they address central issues. There may be a temptation to under-staff the team – a move popular with those who have severe reservations about any increase in support services staff – which should be resisted in the interests of establishing a professional service.

Context

The personnel policy needs to be set in the context of the whole college mission in which people are explicitly valued. That is not to imply that hard, complex decisions are avoided or ducked, or that managers do not recognise their responsibilities. Rather it is demonstrated through managers' actions that the college is fair, reasonable, thorough, open, and listens to comment and criticism in making decisions which affect people. Managers should, and should be seen to give, personnel issues sustained and systematic attention.

The overall purpose of colleges is to bring about change and development on the part of students. To fulfil that objective effectively, colleges must give high priority to developing their own staff. The personnel policy is a key ingredient in doing so. The Department of Employment initiative *Investors in People*, recognises and accredits those organisations who are seen to systematically and comprehensively invest in their staff – colleges should be seen to be at the forefront in that aim.

References

Duckett, Ian (1990) **Piloting appraisal**. Barnet College Publications

Barnet College (1989) **Pilot appraisal scheme: notes for guidance** Barnet College Publications

Health and Safety at Work Act 1974.

Chapter 5: Finance

Peter Briggs
Principal Finance Officer
Leeds Polytechnic

Introduction

At the time of writing Leeds Polytechnic is preparing its third set of statutory accounts since incorporation in April 1989.

Looking back over the last three years the institution's approach to finance has been a major contributory factor to the successful development of the new higher education corporation. The importance of establishing an effective finance function was recognised at an early date by the polytechnic's senior management and initial planning, particularly systems strategies, concentrated on the needs of the finance function.

The objectives of the new corporate colleges are likely to be wide-ranging, covering a series of goals, not all of which are financial targets. However, the opportunities created by corporate status can only be harnessed effectively if the financial structure of the college is properly established at the start.

This chapter attempts to identify those issues that need to be considered as part of the development of the college's strategy in order that a secure financial base can be established at an early stage.

Scope of the finance section

The powers conferred on colleges by corporate status have significant implications for the scope of the finance function after incorporation. As a result colleges need to consider whether they have, or can acquire, adequate resources (human, systems etc.) to satisfactorily respond to these implications. Consideration should also be given to the extent to which the finance functionality can be addressed by the college.

Powers of the new colleges

Corporate status confers on colleges powers to:

- employ their own staff;
- enter into contracts on their own behalf;
- manage assets and resources; and
- act as a legal body undertaking activities in furtherance of their purposes as providers of education.

(DES *et al* 1991)

Employment of staff

The employment of staff, particularly the payment of staff, is one of the most, if not the most, important responsibility of the college. Nothing else can be quite so demoralising and disruptive as a payroll delay.

Leeds Polytechnic placed particular emphasis on its approach to the payment of staff and chose to administer its own personnel and payroll functions with a payroll bureau to process the actual payroll payments. The local authority had previously operated decentralised personnel and payroll processes in various departments but the polytechnic's decision to completely control these functions necessitated extensive consultation with the local authority and the tax and pension bodies in order to ensure that systems and procedures were properly established.

An early decision was taken to reimburse all staff expenses claims through creditor payments, rather than through payroll, leading to a significant reduction in payment delays which again, was judged to be an important priority.

Contract negotiation

Colleges are unlikely to have immediate access to legal and contractual expertise and yet will need to consider whatever income they can earn from full-cost courses, consultancy and other services (DES *et al* 1991).

In order to properly safeguard the financial position of the college it is vital that a sound approach to new contract negotiation is adopted. This particular aspect is covered in more detail in chapter 7 on marketing.

Asset management

The college will be responsible for holding, managing and maintaining all those assets transferred from the former controlling local authority. Asset management in its widest sense is at the very heart of an effective finance function covering not just asset security but also planning, budgeting and monitoring of asset deployment.

A legal entity

The college must ensure that the correct corporate financial structure is established in order to maximise the benefits of the new status conferred by incorporation.

The college, in acting as a charitable body undertaking activities in furtherance of its purpose as a provider of education, is free to engage in educational activities, or activities that are judged to be incidental to the supply of education, with no corporation tax liabilities. However, if the college engages in non-educational, or trading activities, tax liabilities will accrue unless the college establishes a trading company to handle such activities.

Approach to the finance function

As a result of the powers identified above the scope of the finance function in the college is likely to widen considerably. Prior to incorporation most colleges will have some involvement in the local authority's financial processes to a greater or lesser extent. It is certainly true that, as a result of the introduction of delegated budgets, many colleges will enter the new sector with a better understanding of budgetary control than was generally the case with polytechnics in April 1989.

The experience of delegated budget responsibility will have given colleges a taste of the possibilities for development free from the suffocating financial régime operated by local authorities.

However, corporate status will require a further development of the college finance function. Consequently, the first decision that the college must consider is what approach should be adopted to finance? Will the college attempt to address all its finance responsibilities in-house or will part, or all, of these responsibilities be sub-contracted to a third party?

Some of the advantages and disadvantages of an in-house and sub-contracted approach are listed below.

In-house

Advantages

- an in-house approach to finance is likely to be cheaper than most sub-contracting options;

- an in-house approach enables the college to build up expertise in financial matters and to retain this expertise for future development;

- having the finance function controlled in-house allows the college to exercise greater control over the direction of the function thus ensuring greater responsiveness to changing circumstances;

- staff involved in an in-house finance function are likely to show greater loyalty and commitment to the college than that shown by any sub-contractor.

Disadvantages

- an in-house approach to finance is likely to present a steep learning curve for college finance staff, thus increasing pressure on staff at an already pressurised time i.e. incorporation;

- colleges may find it difficult to recruit sufficient suitably qualified staff;

- colleges may consider that the short timescale involved in the incorporation process rules out the development of all aspects in-house.

Sub-contracting part or all of the finance function

Advantages

- by sub-contracting part or all of the finance function the college will be able to concentrate on other priorities for 1st April 1993;

- sub-contracting enables the college to utilise specialist expertise;

- sub-contracting provides a means for colleges and/or polytechnics to work with each other in the provision of common services.

Disadvantages

- sub-contracting is likely to be an expensive method of performing day-to-day finance functions;

- colleges who sub-contract all or part of their finance function will be less able to exercise day-to-day control over the development of these elements.

After a detailed consideration of the possible approaches identified above Leeds Polytechnic opted for an in-house development of its finance function supplemented by specialist consultancy advice on tax planning (corporation tax and VAT) and debt recovery procedures.

Initial planning was concentrated on a staged approach to financial objectives. The first priority was to establish an effective payroll operation together with a basic financial system that guaranteed institutional financial control.

Having achieved the initial objectives Leeds has now begun to develop other financial objectives; a full scheme of financial devolution was introduced from August 1990 and a course costing system from August 1991.

The successful college will be the one that has a measured strategy to the implementation of financial objectives and a clear set of priorities. For most colleges there is insufficient time between now and 1st April 1993 to fully develop all the systems and procedures that will need to be in place in due course. The successful college will have established a hierarchy of objectives, will be aiming to implement the 'essential' objectives for 1st April 1993 and will have a realistic timescale for the delivery of 'highly desirable', 'desirable' and 'cosmetic' objectives over the next couple of years.

Functional considerations

Whatever approach the college adopts to finance there is likely to be an increased workload in all the major functional areas described below.

Accounting framework

Accounting framework is the term given to the coding and reporting structure used in the financial system as well as the definition of the periods to be used for budgets and actual transactions.

Local authority accounting is based on guidelines laid down by the Chartered Institute of Public Finance and Accountancy (CIPFA). In particular, the coding systems used are based on CIPFA's standard classification of income and expenditure.

In determining the appropriate coding structure to be adopted for corporate status the college will need to consider the following:

- the recommended accounting policies for the FE sector;

- the classification of income and expenditure that will be required in statutory accounts;

- the information requirements of the Further Education Funding Council (FEFC) (strategic plans, financial forecasts, mid-year updates of financial forecasts, and statistical information i.e. the equivalent of the PCFC's finance record); and

- the internal information requirements of college management.

It is likely that the accounting policies for the FE sector will match those laid down by the PCFC. If this is the case it is unlikely that the CIPFA standard coding classification will be the most appropriate for the college for two reasons. Firstly, the CIPFA classification provides a breakdown of expenditure into several categories – premises, supplies and services, transport, establishment expenses *et al*. The PCFC accounting policies request information not by type of expenditure but by spending area – academic departments, academic support, administration and central services, premises *et al*.

Secondly, local authority accounting places too much emphasis on different codes for almost every conceivable item of expenditure and income. Such an approach engenders a preoccupation with small sums of money which mitigates against effective budgetary control.

For these reasons Leeds Polytechnic has adopted a much simplified coding structure and groups income and expenditure into more appropriate categories.

Consideration needs to be given to an appropriate reporting structure although, given the flexibility of modern accounting software, it should be possible to aggregate financial information in different structures with different levels of detail. The college's management structure will be replicated in the financial system as the backbone of any reporting structures and it is therefore, essential that such a structure is capable of responding to all the information requirements identified above.

Finally, the college will be in a position to determine the frequency with which it reports financial information internally. The most suitable time period for budget monitoring reports is monthly with shorter timescales for miscellaneous analyses, e.g. cash flow profiles need to be produced on a weekly basis. However, it is advisable to consider the production of periodic reviews of the college's financial position in addition to a regular monthly review, e.g. a half-yearly review or a term-end review.

In each of the three areas mentioned i.e. coding structures, reporting structures and accounting periods, the college will be in the unusual position of being able to determine what structures and periods are most appropriate for its needs. The most important factor that must be borne in mind in making decisions is that the college's future information needs are likely to be very different from the type of service that it receives from its local authority and consequently, serious thought needs to be given to an accounting framework that is more appropriate to those future needs.

Payment of creditors

Two factors need to be held in tension in order to ensure that the college's creditor payments function operates effectively.

Firstly, in order to maximise the cash position of the college, it is vital that no creditor invoices are paid before the appropriate date for payment as laid down in the particular creditor's payment terms.

Secondly, it is vital that the college maintains a reputation for being a good payer in order that future supplies can be secured, when required, at a reasonable price.

Most colleges will be familiar with the process of creditor payment adopted by the local authority and will be involved in some, if not all, of the process.

In considering the best approach to payment of creditors the most important thing is to ensure that a satisfactory level of internal control is built into all stages of the procurement process either by computerised checks or by some other means, for example, paper-based systems.

College orders need to be properly authorised, creditor invoices can only be paid if cross-referenced to authorised orders and there has to be an effective system of certifying that goods have been received.

For all colleges the most efficient way of paying creditors will be through the creation of a creditor payments team who would have the responsibility of generating the final payment to the creditor although staff in the procuring departments in different colleges may have a different amount of involvement with the actual payment process.

In all but the smallest colleges the payment of creditors will be computerised and if payment is to be by cheque (the best method, at least in the early years of corporate life) serious consideration should be given to obtaining a cheque-writing facility, using pre-signed cheques, to avoid the need for staff to be constantly seeking authorising signatures on manually written cheques.

In May 1989 Leeds Polytechnic's creditors section proudly generated its first computerised cheque run which produced 12 cheques. Weekly runs now regularly produce over 300 cheques.

Raising of accounts and debt collection

Payment of debtor invoices is, after funding from the FEFC, likely to be the next most important source of income for the college.

In view of this, and of the likely increase in the proportion of college income that will be generated by fees in future years, it is vital that the college sets up and maintains an effective debt collection section.

Clear principles need to be set out on the payment terms to be adopted by the college e.g. will the use of instalment and credit card payments improve the 'collectability' of debt? Legal advice should be sought on the various stages of legal action that can be taken in order to recover debt; reminders, solicitors' letters, court action etc.

An aged debt analysis should be constantly maintained and monitored to ensure that outstanding debt is minimised and clear instructions should be issued to all staff responsible for raising debt on the documentation that the college requires in order to substantiate the raising of any debt. A clear write-off policy is also required where debts become uncollectable.

As debt collection becomes a higher priority for Leeds Polytechnic attempts are being made to speed up the process of raising accounts, particularly in relation to tuition fees. Use is currently made of a relational database to use student enrolment data in the study information database to generate debtor invoices from the finance database. All possible technology developments need to be explored by colleges in order to ensure that income systems continue to operate at maximum efficiency.

General ledger

Input to the local authority's financial system is probably still by batch processing to a mainframe computer although some local authorities have moved to some of the more recently developed processing systems.

If the college purchases its own financial system it is likely to acquire a system with on-line processing of input as opposed to batch processing. The technical control of all postings to the college's general ledger is likely to represent a new area of responsibility for the college. Consideration needs to be given to the controls that need to be built in; to the period end roll forwards and to the access rights granted in the system.

Even if the college considers that the existing service it receives from the local authority is not suitable, and that the authority's computer system is too inflexible, it is vital that any new system it purchases is properly controlled. All postings to the ledgers should be in accordance with a pre-determined posting timetable. The responsibility for checking that all data has been correctly input to the system needs to be clearly allocated to a person/section. Regular checks on data integrity need to be performed – do the accounts balance?

Consideration also needs to be given to the checks that can be built into any system to highlight exceptions, mis-postings and mis-codings and, if possible, to methods of prevention as well as detection.

All these functions are vital if the mechanics of the college's ledgers are to operate smoothly.

Bank reconciliation

The experience of many institutions in the polytechnic sector in the initial years of corporate status was one of difficulties experienced in account reconciliation procedures of which the main problem area was bank reconciliation.

Entries through the colleges's bank account are likely to be many and consideration needs to be given to the approach to bank reconciliation. Software packages are available to assist in this area but may not be able to cope either with the complexity of the account (due to the number of non-standard transactions processed through the college bank account) or with the specific information needs of the college e.g. how should a receipt be matched and recorded in the college general ledger?

Although Leeds Polytechnic makes use of its bankers' magnetic tape-based bank reconciliation facility much of this process still requires manual analysis yet this is an area that has been highlighted by the polytechnic's auditors as vital to the smooth running of the institution.

Internal audit

Internal audit is judged by the PCFC to be a vital area for polytechnics and all the indications are that this same view is shared by the FEFC.

The FEFC will be conducting a review of the critical financial controls operating in the FE sector in the period leading up to incorporation. Such a review, intended to give the FEFC confidence that all institutions are fitted to receive public funding, will identify the financial controls in operation in each college and establish an action plan for the filling of any gaps identified.

One of the key financial controls to be reviewed is likely to be the internal audit function of the college.

In the case of the polytechnic sector each institution was required to satisfy the PCFC that it had established, or was attempting to establish, a satisfactory internal audit function and that there was an audit committee of the board of governors in place to review the work of this function.

Internal audit is one of the finance functions that could be sub-contracted to an outside body, either to the local authority, to district audit or to a firm of accountants. However, an in-house audit section does provide a valuable resource to the finance division particularly when new systems and procedures are being considered.

Whatever approach is adopted to internal audit the section/unit needs to be clearly independent of the normal line management processes and to have a clear channel of communication to the senior management of the college and the board of governors.

Payroll

Whether or not the college decides to process its payroll in-house, or to sub-contract all or part of the function to a third party, e.g. the local authority or a payroll bureau, consideration needs to be given to the interface of the payroll data with the financial accounts. The decision about what level of detail is required in the financial system is likely to impact not only upon the complexity of the payroll accounting function but also on the performance of the financial system because detailed payroll data has an unnerving ability to clog up systems.

Payroll administration is another area where consultancy advice could prove invaluable to the college particularly in relation to the conduct of PAYE administration. Care is also required to ensure that the tax treatment of staff expenses, self-employed individuals, visiting lecturers and part-time staff is correctly understood.

Financial and management accounts

Colleges will have to prepare statutory accounts for submission to the FEFC on an annual basis. Such accounts will follow the recommended accounting policies that will ultimately be published by the FEFC but the policies will be based on the requirements of the Companies Acts.

A key part of the functionality of the college's finance division is the production of regular budget monitoring information i.e. management accounts to appropriate management levels. Senior management, together with the college governors, will be concerned about the overall financial position of the college and will require regular reports of actual performance against budget. Budget managers throughout the college will also require regular reports but at a more detailed level.

Consideration needs to be given to the relationship between financial and management accounts so that both internal and external reporting of results presents a common picture of the financial state of affairs of the college.

The production and interpretation of financial and management accounts are likely to involve staff at all levels and in all areas of the college and will present a significant challenge to the college's finance division. Effective channels of communication will need to be established and the finance division should be encouraged to take a pro-active role to ensure that all staff within the college fully understand what is required of them.

Value Added Tax

The White Paper 1 points out that colleges will no longer benefit from the unique VAT status of local authorities when they become free standing bodies. Under the existing structure VAT can be largely ignored by colleges as it does not represent a real cost to the institution and neither does the college have to complete VAT returns.

Corporate colleges will have to register for VAT, maintain proper VAT accounting records and complete quarterly VAT returns to HM Customs and Excise.

By the nature of their supplies polytechnics and colleges are extremely complex VAT traders, having a mixture of taxable, exempt, partially exempt and outside the scope activities.

As part of the preparation for corporate status the college will need to review all the supplies it makes in order to assess the VAT treatment of each one. In addition, systems and procedures will need to be set in place to ensure that all new supplies made by the college are properly classified for VAT purposes.

HM Customs and Excise have published guidelines for the application of VAT to universities and polytechnics and these could initially be used as a model by FE colleges.

However, care is needed to ensure that the college properly identifies the VAT liability of all its supplies in order to avoid any of the significant penalties and interest charges that could be levied by HM Customs and Excise if any mistakes are made.

Commitment accounting

Most colleges will already have extensive knowledge of the workings of a commitment accounting system. Commitment accounting records have been commonly kept in local government departments, particularly the education departments, for some years now and have provided a means of accountability for local budget managers to counterbalance inherent data delays in local authority batch processing mainframe accounting applications.

The use of new accounting software packages is replacing batch processing to the extent that there may no longer be significant delays in the production of accounting information. In addition, the creditor payment profile of the college may be better or faster than the local authority, hence, one of the main justifications for commitment accounting is largely removed.

Another important consideration is the amount of administrative effort that could be expended in the maintenance of commitment records compared to the proportion of the college's budget that is actually covered by such records, probably 20 per cent at the very most. Consequently, if the college is faced with limited administrative resources it may consider the prioritisation of other developments rather than commitment accounting, for example, the development of accurate manpower cost reporting systems.

However, if the college operates a commitment accounting system at present and this is familiar to staff throughout the institution, any move away from such a system in future will only render real savings in administrative effort if staff can be persuaded not to substitute manual, or locally developed commitment systems, to replace the system that has been withdrawn.

System strategy

An appropriate system strategy is crucial if the college's road to incorporation is to be a relatively smooth one. A good strategy will enable the college to operate effectively whereas a poor strategy could seriously undermine the process of incorporation.

The college needs to consider its management information needs in respect of all activities, not just finance related activities, although the first priority must be to have a finance system operating for 1st April 1993.

Before an appropriate strategy can be finalised the college needs to be able to define its management information requirements. This definition of requirements is by no means an easy task particularly because colleges are having to make assumptions about their information needs against an uncertain future. However, the college's system strategy **must** be built upon the information requirements of the institution rather than built around hardware or software restrictions.

In defining information requirements the college needs also to bear in mind the need for flexibility in systems. The future information needs of colleges will be very different to their needs in the last year under local authority control. Also, the FEFC are still considering their information requirements from the FE sector for the future. It is likely that FE colleges will be requested to submit strategic plans, financial forecasts and mid-year updates to the FEFC in similar formats to those requested by the PCFC from the PCFC sector. However, discussions have only just begun on the statistical requirements of the FEFC and this will not be completed in time for incorporation. Therefore, flexibility in the college's system strategy is required.

As with the approach to the finance function itself the college has three options to choose from for the procurement of an appropriate finance system. These are: to purchase a software package that has already been developed; to develop an appropriate package in-house; or to sub-contract part/whole of the accounting system.

Unfortunately, there is no one single systems solution that will satisfy the needs of all institutions in the FEFC and PCFC sectors. The solutions chosen by colleges will reflect the different needs and objectives of the colleges and so therefore, it is difficult to generalise about ideal solutions. However, one thing is certainly true: in-house development of systems may appear to be the most attractive because such solutions can be tailored to match the exact requirements of the college but in-house systems development has the longest implementation timescale of the options identified above.

Defining the relationship between the finance division and the institution

Consideration needs to be given to the working relationship that is to be established between the college's finance division and the institution as a whole particularly in respect of financial planning, budget setting and budget monitoring.

What sort of role should the finance division of the corporate college maintain? What approach should be adopted to resource allocation?

One approach is for the college to adopt a structure in which financial control is exercised exclusively in the centre with little delegation of responsibility to managers throughout the college. Alternatively the college could adopt a structure in which little effective control is exercised in the centre and almost all financial responsibility is delegated to other managers.

In practice Leeds Polytechnic has gradually changed its financial structure over the period since incorporation. In the first year most of the polytechnic's budgets were controlled centrally with minimal (approximately two per cent of the total budget and centralised financial processing) delegation of budget responsibility to other managers. In the second year the polytechnic implemented a scheme of devolved budget responsibility – approximately 90 per cent of the total budget with decentralised financial processing.

In the devolved budget environment the role of the finance division is to assist the various budget managers to control and monitor their budgets.

Consideration needs to be given to the appropriate levels of expertise to be lodged in different areas of the college. If the college is to operate a scheme of financial devolution with decision-making extended to other managers what level of support will be given to these managers? Will financial staff be employed directly by the budget centres or will all accounting expertise be lodged in the centre? In practice, a combination of these two is likely to be the best solution. There will be a need to document the financial structure within which the finances of the college will be administered.

The college will require its own set of financial regulations which will need to be approved by its board of governors. Such a document will spell out the financial responsibilities of the governors, senior officers and all polytechnic staff and state clearly what responsibilities need to be carried out and how frequently.

In addition it would be advisable for the college to produce a set of financial procedures to spell out precisely how the responsibilities set out in financial regulations should be carried out. With all such documents great care needs to be exercised by the finance division to ensure that procedural requirements are regularly and effectively communicated to all college staff.

Whatever financial structure is adopted it is crucial that all staff at all levels are clear about the decision-making hierarchy within the college.

Conclusion

The success of the corporate college will be determined to a large extent by the effectiveness with which it establishes its financial structure. The financial implications of incorporation are wide-ranging and there are many tasks to be fulfilled in order to have an adequately staffed, prepared and resourced finance function in place for 1st April 1993.

Clarity is required about how many of these tasks really can be accomplished in the timescale available, about which of the tasks are essential and which only desirable and about the overall system strategy of the college.

Realistic planning, with achievable objectives, is essential in order to ensure that the college is able to cope with the new powers that corporate status confers upon it.

Reference

Department of Education and Science *et al* (1991) **Education and training for the 21st century.** Cm 1536 Volume I. Cm 1536 Volume II. HMSO

Chapter 6: Quality assurance

Margaret Jack
Director, Quality Assurance and Control, BTEC
and
Paul Sokoloff
Manager, Validation, BTEC

Introduction

The 1990s are being heralded as 'the decade of quality, access and value for money, for further and higher education.' The past 10 years have seen an unprecedented increase in the number of students staying on in education post-16. Throughout that time the Government has continuously pressed for reductions in unit cost;, access and value for money have been paramount. The reality of low cost mass further and higher education has turned the focus on to quality.

It could be held that a higher unit of resource leads to improved quality. As early as 1983 the HMI (Her Majestys Inspectorate) report on degree courses, entitled **100 degree courses in higher education: an HMI commentary** (HMI 1983), made it clear that the provision of resources did not guarantee quality and that quality did not necessarily increase with resources. Nevertheless, amongst professionals working in education there is an underlying belief that there is a clear relationship between quality and resources and that if resources are reduced significantly then the result will be lower quality. This suggested relationship has not been proved and the Government is determined to obtain the highest quality education at the lowest possible cost. Those within education are faced with the problem of maintaining quality in a period of reducing unit costs.

The change from an élite to a mass system of post-16 education poses another problem for quality. In our traditionally élite system, quality had much to do with reputation and standards, and informal pressures from within the institutions were usually sufficient to deal with situations where reputation was seriously threatened by falling standards. When an élite system of education changes to a mass system funded on a competitive basis these ideals of internal pressure and self-regulation are no longer sufficient. A mass system which has a broad spectrum of students with varying backgrounds and aims is inevitably more diverse and provides a much greater range of opportunities. In these circumstances quality can no longer be related to a single standard as it has been in the relatively homogenous élite system of the past.

Quality and its definitions

But what is quality? It is often said that quality is easy to recognise but difficult to define. Those involved with manufacturing industry will generally give a definition which refers to reliability, performance, a known high standard, good management or customer care. Fitness for purpose is a favourite phrase. Why buy a Rolls Royce when a Mini will do? However, in education it appears to be a much more elusive and controversial concept. Pirsig in his **Zen and the art of motorcycle maintenance** (1974) expresses the problem well:

> Quality: we know what it is, yet we don't know what it is. But that is self-contradictory, for some things are better than others: that is, they have more quality. But when you try to say what the quality is, apart from the things that have it, it all goes 'poof'. There's nothing to talk about. But if you can't say what quality is, how do you know what it is, or how do you know that it even exists? If no one knows what it is, then for all practical purpose, it doesn't exist at all. But for all practical purposes it really does exist. What else are the grades based on? Why else would people pay fortunes for some things and throw others in the trash pile? So round and round you go, spinning mental wheels, and nowhere finding any place to get traction. What the hell is quality? What is it?
> (Pirsig 1974)

If quality is impossible to define, how can it be either assured or measured and what is the purpose of wishing to do the latter? In trying to answer these questions one is automatically drawn back to the concept of fitness for purpose and hence institutional mission. A college may turn out high quality footballers, for example, but is that an intended purpose? Colleges need to start out with a clear mission or vision about what they are hoping to achieve, against which the quality of their output can ultimately be judged.

Quality assurance

In higher education circles the concept of quality assurance is now well established. It is widely acknowledged that quality is best assured by self-evaluation in a situation where:

- everyone in the college has a responsibility for **maintaining** the quality of the product or service (i.e. the sub-standard rarely reaches the quality controllers because they have been rejected at source), everyone in the college has a responsibility for **enhancing** the quality of the product or service;

– everyone in the college understands, uses and feels ownership of the systems which are in place for **maintaining** and **enhancing** quality; and

– management regularly checks the **validity** and **viability** of the systems for checking quality.

However, it is also accepted that self-evaluation requires:

– information on current (best) practice; and

– that its conclusions are periodically tested by an independent body which has responsibility for ensuring that there are adequate systems of quality assurance across the entire sector.

Quality measurement

The concept of quality measurement is less well understood and even less well accepted. Nevertheless, it is an issue which Government has been determined to tackle in relation to the funding of higher education. Since the establishment of the Polytechnics and Colleges Funding Council (PCFC) in January 1989 there has been an explicit relationship between the amount of funding a college receives for a specified number of students on a particular group of courses and the perceived quality of those courses.

Even though the amount of funds which have been allocated as a direct consequence of quality judgements has been small (less than five per cent of the total funding in any one year) the exercise has been highly controversial. The debate has centred firstly on the very concept of linking funding with quality, and secondly, on the methods which have been used to make these quality judgements (or measurements). Nevertheless, it is interesting to note that the large majority of those institutions which have received an outstanding quality rating in a particular programme area have used this fact to maximum effect in their publicity and recruitment material. Thus, the PCFC's aim of finding a better means to inform student applicants about quality, thereby strengthening the role of student choice in its determining the allocation of funds between institutions, has been achieved.

Up to 1991 the PCFC based its quality judgements on advice from two sources. The first and more important of these is HMI who use a five point scale described as follows:

– generally good, or with some outstanding features or with many good features;

– some good features and no major shortcomings;

- sound but undistinguished, no significant extremes, or good features balanced by shortcomings;

- some shortcomings in important areas;

- many shortcomings, generally poor.

HMI place a group of related courses in an institution into one of these categories on the basis of their (infrequent) inspections and their own professional judgement. HMI claim that these judgements are tempered, refined and reinforced by continual cross-fertilisation with colleagues within and across specialist HMI teams. Though built up from the opinions of individual inspectors, the overall evaluation offered is a collective HMI view and there is no formal opportunity for institutions to discuss the ratings with HMI before they are passed to PCFC. The second source of advice is that which (for non-degree courses) is offered by BTEC (Business and Technology Education Council). This is based on the structured and systematic information collected by BTEC moderators during the course of their regular visits to institutions and the findings of the monitoring exercises. All the information which contributes to the overall judgement has already been shared with institutions and the judgement itself is cleared with the institution before it is passed to PCFC.

Any system of quality measurement is likely to arouse suspicion and create controversy particularly in those institutions which fail to gain a high rating. It is important, therefore, that the system used is open and explicit and allows those involved to question and challenge the judgements which are made. The principles of quality measurement must follow those which have already been accepted in respect of quality assurance – that those involved in the delivery of the course are best placed to make judgements about its quality.

Quality and funding – the future

The question which now arises is will the Government's emphasis on quality measurement and its relationship with funding wither, or will it continue as a major element of future policy? The signs are that it will continue. In a recent National Audit Office report (1991) on the PCFC the following paragraphs are worthy of note:

the National Audit Office endorse the underlying concepts implicit in this funding methodology which recognises the importance of student demand, price and quality of educational provision (Para 7)

the quality of educational provision, including teaching, is rewarded in the funding process (Para 18).
(National Audit Office 1991)

The Report draws attention however, to the continued absence of performance indicators of both the quality and quantity of teaching within institutions. The definition of good teaching and learning and the associated performance indicators are concepts with which many have grappled but have as yet failed to specify. One of the most recent attempts was by the PCFC itself which set up a committee of enquiry, chaired by Baroness Warnock, to identify characteristics of effective and efficient teaching which could be developed as indicators of teaching quality. The Committee in its report **Teaching quality: report of the committee of enquiry** of October 1990 concluded that there were five necessary conditions, which are not sufficient in themselves, but which must be fulfilled before teaching can be good. These are:

- clarity of aims and objectives;
- a curriculum organisation and delivery policy which includes effective methods of promoting learning;
- a policy for the professional development of teaching staff, including appointment, induction, appraisal and development;
- means of involving student and employer views in judging the curriculum, its delivery and outcomes; and
- a framework for institutional self-evaluation.

Yet again the need for a comprehensive framework and a process which draws upon self and peer evaluation come through very strongly as essential elements of a quality system.

The White Papers and quality

The two recent education White Papers published in 1991 (DES *et al* 1991a and 1991b) have much to say on quality. **Higher education – a new framework** states that :

> The prime responsibility for maintaining and enhancing the quality of teaching and learning rests with each individual institution. At the same time, there is a need for proper accountability for the substantial public funds invested in higher education. As part of this, students and employers need improved information about quality if the full benefit of increased competition is to be obtained.
> (DES *et al* 1991a)

This White Paper introduces two new terms into the already confused world of quality. The first is quality audit which it describes as a means of checking that relevant systems and structures within an institution support its key teaching mission. It is proposed that the quality audit role should become the task of a newly established unit in which institutions have the major stake. The second is quality assessment. This is described as arrangements to assess the quality of what is actually provided so that this can continue to inform the funding decisions of the new Funding Councils. It is stated that there are two ways in which quality assessments should be developed. The first is to be through quantifiable outcomes – performance indicators and calculations of value added will have an important role to play. The second approach is to be through external judgement on the basis of direct observation of what is provided. Again a separate unit will be established to take on this role, but this time under the umbrella of the Funding Councils.

The FE White Paper, **Education and training for the 21st century** (DES *et al* 1991b) has less to say about quality. This might be interpreted as an indication that the existing thinking and systems are less well developed than those in higher education. The document opens the section on quality by stating:

> The Government attaches great importance to systems which will ensure the quality of education and training provided by the colleges. Responsibilities for monitoring and assessing quality in the new sectors need to be clearly defined.
> (DES *et al* 1991b)

It then goes on to say that each college will have primary responsibility for its own quality control and will need to implement effective systems to improve its quality and contribute to its own efficiency and effectiveness. The White Paper is also clear that the examining and validating bodies will be responsible for guaranteeing the quality of the qualifications offered in the colleges. In large part this describes the position as it currently exists except that it is perhaps the first time that the Government has been so explicit in stating that it is the FE and sixth form colleges themselves that must accept this responsibility, following the lead taken by the HE sector. The only piece of new thinking in the FE White Paper in respect of quality is in the small section on external assessment. At the moment it is claimed that the two main sources of this external assessment are Her Majesty's Inspectorate and the LEA advisers. In the future it is intended that the FEFC will have responsibility for:

– ensuring that quality systems in general form a satisfactory basis for the funding being provided – responsibility for quality flows from responsibility for finance; and

– making specific financial allocation decisions which should be informed by quality judgements.

In other words the Government intends that the FEFC will follow the lead of PCFC and use quality as an explicit criterion in the funding formula.

Government departments and quality

The 1991 education White Papers (DES *et al* 1991a and 1991b) set out Government thinking about quality from the Department of Education and Science perspective, but does this sit comfortably with that coming from other government departments? The National Council for Vocational Qualifications (NCVQ) whose funding comes directly from the Department of Employment appears to relate quality directly to the achievement of outcomes, through the assessment of competence. Thus the NCVQ's quality assurance requirements are directed primarily at awarding bodies and place on them the obligation to ensure that

- institutional assessment procedures are rigorous, valid and reliable; and
- institutional assessors and internal verifiers are trained to the appropriate national standard and act in an objective and consistent way.

The NCVQ system does not explicitly embrace the quality of the learning experience which in the eyes of many educators and employers is fundamental to the achievement of a high quality outcome.

The Training and Enterprise Councils (TECs) which are also funded via the Department of Employment tend to view quality from a manufacturing industry standpoint and have put a great deal of emphasis on frameworks such as BS 5750 (or its international equivalent ISO 9000), total quality management (TQM) or even strategic quality management (SQM).

Quality frameworks

A number of colleges have started to look at these various frameworks in detail and a few have already achieved registration against BS 5750. But what does this mean? Does it for instance guarantee that every individual who completes a programme at that particular college will be able to perform at a specified level? This is certainly not the case. Registration against a national standard guarantees little except that the organisation concerned has put an enormous amount of time, effort and money into specifying procedures for every activity covered by the registration, in which the organisation is involved. However, if the writing of procedures is approached in a positive way the very discipline of involving all staff in the process can be extremely powerful and beneficial.

All this leads back to the view that quality can only be assured where there is ownership, responsibility, accountability, commitment and public scrutiny. Accordingly TQM, which has been described as 'a way of managing to improve the responsiveness, effectiveness, flexibility and competitiveness of the college as a whole', is a much more appropriate framework. TQM is about changing the culture of an organisation so that everyone working in it whether they be principal, lecturer, cleaner or secretary feels responsible for the quality of the product or service. TQM cannot happen overnight: it needs a set of conditions to develop and evolve which include:

- a commitment at top level;
- an awareness of the college's mission, values and goals by all who work in the college;
- teamwork across and between all levels;
- a commitment to continuous improvement;
- simple procedures which are owned by those who operate them;
- a commitment to an investment in staff development and training.

Quality and Europe

The principles of peer review and evaluation which have been developed so extensively in British higher education are likely to be adopted on a Europe-wide basis in the near future. Education ministers from the 12 member states have recently agreed the need for a European 'quality assessment experience' to complement national systems. The European Commission is to conduct a comparative study of national assessment methods by the end of 1992, and will examine the feasibility of pilot projects to develop 'instruments' for strengthening quality evaluation on a European level. It has been agreed that these should take account of practical experience of systems such as the British model of peer review visiting teams.

Challenges

While sixth form and tertiary colleges are, with some exceptions, relative newcomers to vocational post-16 education with their cultures mostly influenced by the schools sector, the further education colleges have a long history and a robust attitude to survival. Most FE colleges have offered a staggering range of subjects and levels to meet the needs of the local community. The student body is usually diverse in age profile, background and motivation; the pattern of course provision is such that day release, evening classes and short courses may predominate over the full-time mode; the teaching day often extends over 12 or more hours and the proportion of part-time staff employed may be considerable.

These very strengths of the FE system have proved a powerful barrier to the adoption of a college-wide approach to quality management. Departments have developed with a considerable degree of independence and autonomy, and often take a somewhat insular view of their activities. Individual staff, particularly part-timers, have seen themselves as subject specialists serving a narrow range of interests, with little allegiance to the wider college aims. This has led to a wide range of working practices within a single institution. Responsibility for quality has been seen to lie outside the college with external awarding bodies determining whether or not a course should be allowed to operate and setting out rigid rules and regulations and monitoring the operation of courses. These difficulties have been exacerbated by a poorly developed infrastructure for quality management. Formal structures were either non-existent or ineffective, lines of responsibility and accountability were poorly defined, and feedback to staff on quality issues was fragmented.

This bleak picture is partly a caricature of the FE system though many will recognise the elements within it. Nevertheless, until each of the barriers has been recognised and cleared, the chances of success are minimised.

Many colleges have made great strides in recent years to develop a more coherent approach to quality management. This development has been enhanced by factors such as the sharing of work across traditional boundaries, be it FE colleges taking on degree or BTEC HND work from polytechnics, or sixth form colleges offering BTEC First and National awards. Some awarding bodies, notably BTEC, are now placing greater emphasis on the sharing of responsibility for quality assurance, providing college managers with an incentive to strengthen college-wide quality systems.

Towards a practical system

No quality management system can operate effectively without formal structures. No matter how deeply a commitment to quality is embedded within a college, management, control and ultimately credibility can only be achieved by co-ordinating the whole effort in a structured forum which is recognised and accepted by all in the college.

Unfortunately, the word 'committee' can be a barrier to progress. Staff may view committee work as at best irrelevant and at worst a malign intrusion into the business of teaching. Participation is given low priority, and lack of time is normally cited as the reason for non-attendance. Acceptance of formal structures is part of the cultural change needed, and college management can facilitate this change by ensuring that:

- the number of formal committees is as few as is commensurate with the size and diversity of the college;

- each committee should have a clearly defined place within the college structure;

- committees and their work are visible to staff and students;

- the terms of reference, procedures, authority and accountability are clearly laid out;

- any evaluative work carried out by a committee is based upon clear, written criteria;

- no committee meets unless there is a specific job to do.

The simplest functional model for quality management embraces three elements – validation, monitoring and review, and each college should have a clear view on what these elements comprise, and the purpose that they serve. Guiding principles should embrace the following.

Accountability: the college is accountable to a range of stakeholders for the quality of its own courses. This accountability is devolved and shared throughout the college.

Openness and fairness: external participation, peer review and the sharing of outcomes within the college build confidence in the system.

Consistency: the dissemination of information on good practice and the involvement of staff across college boundaries enhances consistency.

Partnership: validation and review are constructive and linked processes designed to ensure that a college achieves its mission in providing a quality service to the community. Although the processes should be thorough and searching, they are not adversarial contests between teachers and managers.

Validation covers all the stages that lead to the approval of a course by the college and, where appropriate, an external body. Early stages in the validation process are informal but should be guided by a college-wide framework which ensures that staff energies are focused on appropriate issues. Later on, the process becomes more formal as the proposals collated by the development team come under scrutiny.

Validation itself applies most properly to new proposals, as the revalidation process is effectively subsumed into the review process. Here a course is subject to a major internal review, say once every five years, which in turn leads to a decision whether or not to continue to offer a course, and if so what changes are required.

Monitoring can be viewed as the systematic gathering of relevant data for use in subsequent review and evaluation. Monitoring is a continuous process, and systems must be in place to capture and hold the data until required.

Review and evaluation relate to a process (review) in which judgements are made using appropriate performance indicators (evaluation) in order to achieve the objectives of the review. It is useful to distinguish between two types of review:

- – frequent review – for example, after each year of a course. This is often referred to as an annual monitoring and may address a fixed agenda each year, for example, admissions, withdrawals, results, destinations, together with specific areas which may change from year to year;

- – a major review after a longer period of time – up to five years – which provides an in-depth perspective on a course, its strengths, weaknesses and future.

Validation, monitoring, frequent review and major review all operate through the formal structures of the college which link the teacher to the governing body through a series of participative and interactive committees.

In **Figure 7** seven types of committee are identified, although for smaller colleges functions can be combined to keep numbers to a manageable level.

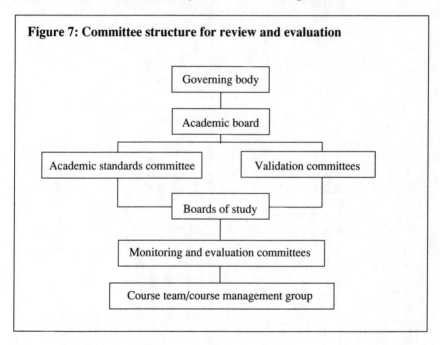

Figure 7: Committee structure for review and evaluation

Governing body

Academic board

Academic standards committee

Validation committees

Boards of study

Monitoring and evaluation committees

Course team/course management group

An example of how these committees might interact in an annual review process is shown in **Figure 8**.

Course team

The course team comprises all staff teaching on a course and, where appropriate, student representation. Where the course team is very large a smaller course

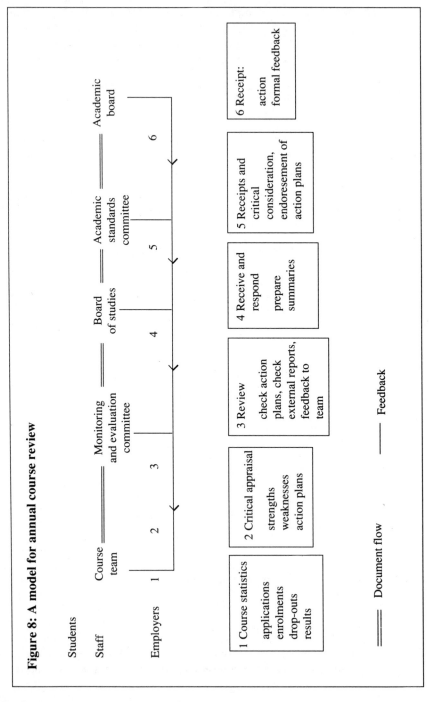

Figure 8: A model for annual course review

management group is often responsible for discharging the formal responsibilities of the team.

The work of teachers is the prime determinant of quality, and therefore it follows that considerable responsibility must be delegated to the course team. These responsibilities must be formally set down, and the committee structure must be seen to be supportive to the professional skills of the teaching staff. The team has two broad areas of responsibility – delivery and monitoring. Delivery covers:

- – implementing college-wide policy on recruitment, admission, induction, learning and assessment;
- – preparing documentation for students – for example study guides;
- – maintaining a general overview of the conduct of the course including its coherence, maintenance of standards, curriculum developments, identification of staff development needs and taking any corrective action that may be necessary.

Monitoring covers:

- – preparing documentation for internal and external validation;
- – writing definitive course documentation;
- – maintaining records relevant to the course;
- – collecting data for monitoring purposes;
- – preparing and presenting an annual course review or monitoring report;
- – preparing documentation for any periodic review of the course.

Course teams would normally be responsible to the head of department for the general management of the course and to the board of studies, via the monitoring and evaluation committee for the maintenance of standards.

Monitoring and evaluation committee

The monitoring and evaluation committee(s) would normally report to the board of Studies, but in smaller colleges a separate committee may not be necessary. Monitoring and review provides a mechanism for peer group review within cognate disciplines. Typical functions might include:

- – scrutinising reports from course teams;
- – offering guidance, support and feedback to course teams on monitoring and evaluation;
- – consulting with management on matters requiring executive action or on matters of concern;

- reporting to the board of studies on quality issues relating to particular courses.

Board of studies

The board of studies may be constituted at a department, school or faculty level and provides the key link with committees dealing with college-wide matters. The board would hold responsibility for standards on courses within its remit, and may act:

- to receive, consider and act upon the reports of the monitoring and review committee;

- to identify and formally report to the head of department on matters of concern relating to particular courses;

- to endorse or prepare formal reports for the academic board or academic standards committee.

Academic standards committee

An academic standards committee may have considerable executive responsibility delegated from the academic board. These responsibilities can be divided into three broad categories – monitoring, advisory and executive. Its functions might include:

- developing policies and procedures and issuing guidelines for the monitoring of course quality;

- ensuring that each department, school or faculty has mechanisms suitable for the effective implementation of college review and evaluation procedures;

- receiving reports from boards of study on course quality, and reporting to the academic board.

The executive function of an academic standards committee may lie in its responsibility for validation issues. Ad hoc sub-groups can act as validation committees to consider proposals for new courses, or the re-approval of existing courses before they are submitted to an external examining or validating body.

Academic board

The academic board must take overall responsibility for quality issues at a college wide level, and:

- receives reports on the monitoring and evaluation process from the academic standards committee;

- takes any necessary action with reference to individual courses or other outcomes of monitoring and evaluation.

Tools for quality management

Committees cannot function effectively without formally agreed:

- terms of reference listing purpose, accountability, authority and principal tasks;

- membership;

- key dates for completion of principal tasks;

- procedures for operation.

All of these take time to develop and refine, but pay dividends in the long run. At the operational level, performance indicators and criteria for quality need to be developed. Although a number of these will be course specific, the majority will be sufficiently generic to apply to all courses and at all levels.

There is very little published material available for reference, but BTEC uses a criterion-referenced system for its own quality assurance and control. This model uses a series of criteria which define quality for a particular issue, and then sets out a list of indicators by which staff can determine the degree to which particular criteria have been met. Many of the indicators are readily convertible to performance indicators. The sources for these criteria for quality are set out in the bibliography,and an example is given in **Figure 9**. This example relates to the physical resources needed to support a course.

Quality control of assessment

Developments in National Vocational Qualifications (NVQs) in all their guises place a considerable emphasis on assessment, and external examining and validating bodies are increasingly focusing their quality checks on the processes and outcomes of assessment within colleges.

Assessment regulations may be imposed by an external agency, and augmented by college-wide policy. Assessment strategy and process are embedded within course validation and review but the quality control of assessment is often overlooked.

At a basic level, the setting and marking of assessments is devolved to the teacher, often with no checks at all on validity and consistency. Folklore about 'tough' markers and 'lenient' markers abounds, but to a quality conscious institution these concepts are an anathema.

Figure 9: Criteria for quality control

At validation:

Criteria	Ways in which the team can demonstrate this
There will be necessary adequate physical resources to support the course	• Details of appropriate capital items, including equipment to support particular parts of the course. • Details of replaceable items (e.g. raw materials, trade journals). • Information on library/learning resources appropriate to the needs of the course.
There will be procedures for replacing and updating resources	• Procedures for replacing/updating resources. • Details of funds available for renewing equipment.
There will be access to the relevant resources by all students.	• Information on the situation and adequate opening times of resource areas. • Evidence to confirm that sufficient resources are available to the course to match the student numbers.

At review each of the criteria is revisited to determine the extent to which the resources have met the needs of the course, and if they will continue to meet these needs – for example, the adequacy of resources needs to be reviewed in terms of their relevance, usage and the degree to which they reflect current industrial practice.

Internal monitoring or verification procedures are essential, but for practical reasons must operate predominantly at the level of the course team. A college should have a policy on internal monitoring, and a procedure for feeding information on monitoring into the formal structure. A useful forum for capturing this data is at the annual course review, although action must be taken immediately if problems are identified during the operation of a course.

The college may, for example, require that for each course:

- there is a named group with responsibility for the internal verification and quality control of assessment;

- the group systematically monitors all aspects of the assessment process;

- the team modifies, as necessary, its assessment practice as a result of the internal monitoring and, where relevant, evidence from external monitoring such as BTEC moderator reports;

- checks are made as to the quality of individual assessments, and corrective action is taken as appropriate;

- student work is systematically sampled and its assessment cross-checked using internal verification processes where appropriate.

Conclusions

There is no doubt that quality will be a major issue for education in the 1990s. Much has already been written about the subject and it is a topic which is currently being debated in respect of every level of education from nursery through to post-graduate studies. However, commitment to quality requires the allocation of resources – particularly staff time.

Quality in today's world of education cannot be defined in absolute terms and must be related to fitness for purpose and institutional mission. In further education the words of Sheila Browne (1984), written in 1984 as the Head of HM Inspectorate, still seem the most appropriate.

> The real evidence of quality lies in the subsequent performance (in employment) of the student and in the skills and knowledge which remain at his or her disposal.
> (Browne 1984)

The colleges themselves must accept the primary responsibility for assuring the quality of both their offerings and their outputs. This can only be achieved when everyone in the college acknowledges that they have a responsibility for maintaining and enhancing the quality of the service they provide. To facilitate this there must be a structured and comprehensive system which is open to public scrutiny and which is based upon the principles of self-evaluation, peer review and subsequent action.

However, there is also a need for a national overview through an external quality audit agency. This body would have responsibility for checking that the quality assurance and control processes of individual colleges were appropriate and were working properly.

References

Browne, Sheila (1984) The NAB and 'quality' in higher education. **Higher Education Review** Volume 17, number 1 Autumn 1984, pp 45-50

Booth, B and Booth, C (1989) Planning for quality: advice respectfully tendered to the Polytechnics and Colleges Funding Council. **Higher Education Quarterly** Volume 43 number 4. Autumn 1989, pp 278-88

Business and Technician Education Council (1988) **Course review and evaluation: general guideline.** BTEC

Business and Technology Education Council (1991a) **Guidance for completing application forms for approval.** BTEC

Business and Technician Education Council (1991b) **Handbook for moderators, Part 1: moderation, the role of moderators and associated professional requirements.** BTEC

Department of Education and Science *et al* (1991a) **Higher education – a new framework.** Cm 1541 HMSO

Department of Education and Science *et al* (1991b) **Education and training for the 21st century.** Cm 1536 Volume I. Cm 1536 Volume II. HMSO.

Frazer M (1991) **Quality assurance in higher education.** Paper presented to international conference on quality assurance in higher education in Hong Kong 1991. [unpublished]

Her Majesty's Inspectorate (1983) **Degree courses in the public sector of higher education: an HMI commentary.** HMSO

Her Majesty's Inspectorate (1989) **Quality in higher education: in pursuit of quality: an HMI view.** A report on the HMI invitation conference. HMSO

Miller, J and Dower, A (1989) **Improving quality in further education: a guide for teachers in course teams.** Department of Employment Training Agency.

National Audit Office (1991) **Polytechnics and Colleges Funding Council: report by the Comptroller and Auditor General.** HMSO

Pirsig R M (1974). **Zen and the art of motorcycle maintenance: an inquiry into values.** New York, Morrow

Polytechnics and Colleges Funding Council (1990) **Teaching quality: report of the committee of enquiry: appointed by the council. Chair: Baroness Warnock**

Theodossin, E and Thomson, CE (1987). Performance indicators: theory and practice. **Coombe Lodge Report** Volume 20 Number 1. Blagdon, The Further Education Staff College

Williams G (1990) Quality and resource allocation *in* Loder, C P J (ed) **Quality assurance and accountability in higher education.** Kogan Page

Chapter 7: Marketing

Peter Briggs
Principal Finance Officer
Leeds Polytechnic

Introduction

The 1987 White Paper (DES *et al* 1987) states that 'the Government and its central funding agencies will do all they can to encourage and reward approaches by higher education institutions which bring them closer to the world of business.' The funding model adopted in the PCFC sector has sought to encourage institutions to be less dependent upon direct funding through the PCFC and to generate an increasing proportion of their funds from tuition fees and external income sources.

At the time of writing clarification is still being sought on the likely funding model to be used by the FEFC for the new sector. However, it is likely that funding will have two main components, a recurrent element related to the 1991/92 college budgets and a demand element based on the student numbers of each institution.

Clearly the FE colleges will need to actively market their services in an increasingly competitive environment. This chapter attempts to identify those issues that need to be considered as part of the development of the college's marketing strategy.

Funding methodology

The funding model adopted by the PCFC has evolved gradually over the early years of the sector. Initially PCFC institutions started life with a guaranteed sum from the PCFC for recurrent expenditure, inherited capital liabilities (both staff related and debt charges) and for other specific items e.g. additional funding to cover the cost of irrecoverable VAT.

In 1989/90 funding from the PCFC accounted for 62 per cent of Leeds Polytechnic's total revenue income.

In each successive year the proportion of total polytechnic income received from the PCFC has decreased due to three factors.

Firstly, the 'guaranteed' element of PCFC funding has been diminishing in real terms and is being overtaken by a system of bidding for PCFC funds. Each year polytechnics receive 90 per cent of the previous year's guaranteed sum, the balance of funds being made available to institutions by means of a bidding process.

There are many factors taken into account in this bidding process, price and quantity of provision are not the sole determinants. However, the bidding process itself illustrates the competitive environment within which polytechnics operate and highlights the need for a clear marketing strategy.

Secondly, PCFC funding has been further diminished to compensate for the increased tuition fees that are now chargeable across the HE sector. In 1989/90 the basic fee for a full-time HE course was £607. In the last two years this fee has more than trebled and courses now have a fee band structure.

The vast majority of tuition fees are government funded (indirectly through funding of LEA's mandatory awards) and, as a result of the increased income generated from the higher fees, the level of PCFC funding has been reduced to compensate this fee shift.

Finally, the real unit of resource funded by the PCFC diminishes in each successive year because of the gap between real levels of inflation and pay settlements and the allowances built into funding settlements through the Treasury deflator model. As its name suggests, the Treasury deflator lags behind the effective rate of price increases prevalant in the economy.

Faced with this decrease in funding PCFC institutions have three options: to increase student numbers; to increase income from other sources; or to cut costs.

- Increases in student numbers require careful planning not only to determine what marketing strategy is likely to be successful in attracting new students but also in ensuring that the institution has adequate resources (staff, space) to cope effectively with greater numbers.

- Consultancy, bespoke courses and applied research provide opportunities for institutions to increase total income but not all institutions have the same capacity to capitalise on such markets and the market itself is limited.

- Cuts in expenditure prove difficult to secure particularly in view of the significant proportion of total expenditure that is accounted for by staff costs which are not easily varied.

It is not unreasonable to expect that a similar funding methodology to that employed in the PCFC sector will eventually be developed in the FE sector and that FE colleges will face pressure to become more financially independent. In the light of this, early consideration needs to be given to the best ways in which the college can prepare itself for this new environment and to an appropriate approach for marketing the college.

Components of a marketing strategy

There are three component parts to an institutional marketing strategy: the definition of the mission and objectives of the college; the identification of the college's target market; and the management of the college's contacts with its target market.

Mission objectives

The starting point for any marketing strategy must be a clear definition of the mission of the college which sets out why the college exists and what objectives it is trying to achieve.

Colleges must not lose sight of their main business which is the delivery of quality educational courses to students together with other services incidental to the supply of education. Even though the future funding methodology to be adopted by the FEFC may encourage colleges to generate more income from contacts with the business community, such an objective must not be allowed to unduly influence the overall strategy of the college.

A marketing strategy that concentrates on the peripheral activities of the college e.g. consultancy, and doesn't focus sufficient attention on the delivery of mainstream courses, could place the college in a vulnerable position by diverting attention away from the need to respond to changes in the market place for FE courses.

Equally, a strategy that concentrates entirely on the FE courses to the exclusion of other income generating activities could be equally problematical. If the college does not adequately address the need to develop additional markets then it could well be faced with a reducing unit of resource and no strategy for development of other sources of income.

Target market

Once the mission and objectives of the institution have been decided the college needs to identify the total available markets for its services and specifically, what section or sections of those markets it will seek to address.

Such a consideration needs to take into account the particular strengths and weaknesses of the college in order that the target markets represent realistic opportunities for the college.

In terms of FE courses an objective may be a widening of access to further education through the enrolment of a greater number of mature students or a broadening of the market through the recruitment of overseas students but in both areas the college will need to provide specialist facilities to cater for the particular and very different needs of these two groups of students.

In terms of other activities the initial strategy will be largely determined by the experience that the college has already had of income generating activities. If this experience is extensive the college will be in a position to seek to expand these activities particularly those that are most genuinely profitable. If the college has had little experience of income generation a suitable portfolio of activities will need to be developed that utilises the best of the college's skills and experience.

In both the above cases a careful review of the total potential market will be required to identify the scope for the college to expand its income. A successful marketing strategy can ultimately create the markets for the college but, in the initial years, such a strategy may be beyond the reaches of most colleges.

Management of contacts

If the college is going to satisfactorily address its target market, consideration needs to be given to mechanisms for managing contacts with the target market.

A marketing strategy does not only involve the publication of glossy literature advertising the courses and facilities that the college can offer but also the management and regular review of contacts in order to ensure that the objectives identified above are achieved.

Particular thought needs to be given to the image which the college wishes to present to its target market. In all cases emphasis needs to be placed on the college's overall mission and objectives as well as the particular benefits that can be offered to different groups of potential customers. A college which has a clear view about its reason for existence and about the facilities it can offer is more likely to be judged successful and worthy of attention than a college which appears vague, inconsistent and uncertain of its role.

Having identified the particular markets that should be developed the college needs to establish processes for monitoring these objectives. Management information systems need to be developed that provide data on the profile of the college's students and, in particular, on noticeable trends in this profile. Reports need to be produced regularly enough to be able to inform decision making processes so that, if the objectives are not being met, remedial action can be taken.

Although one manager may be given the responsibility for the overall implementation of the marketing strategy the strategy itself will actually be implemented by staff across the college. It is not the marketing managers who interface with the outside world on a day-to-day basis but the academic managers, course leaders, consultants etc. As a result, it is vital that the marketing strategy of the college is widely understood throughout the college. All staff should recognise that, as employees of a new corporate body, they are representatives of the college as a whole and should be actively seeking to market all the services of the college, not just the particular services with which they are concerned.

The college may also decide to delegate responsibility for the achievement of particular strategic objectives and for the management of contacts with particular customers e.g. local businesses with a range of managers throughout the institution.

The college company

Colleges will be established as corporate bodies with charitable status. This charitable status derives from the nature of the services that colleges provide i.e. educational services. The college is free to engage in educational activities, or activities that are judged to be incidental to the supply of education, and benefit from charitable status – to suffer no corporation tax liabilities on the income generated from these activities.

However, if the college engages in non-educational, or trading activities, e.g. consultancy, the charitable status of the college will not prevent corporation tax liabilities accruing on such income.

Consequently, if the marketing strategy of the college includes the provision of services likely to be classed as trading activities by the Inland Revenue, then it is vital that an appropriate company is established as a means of avoiding potential corporation tax. All trading activities will be channelled through the trading company (which will probably be a wholly owned subsidiary of the college) and the profits made by the company each year will be covenanted back to the college under deed of covenant transfer.

Such a structure (incidentally, one which was recommended to the PCFC sector by the Inland Revenue themselves) may simply be adopted by the college in order to ensure that corporation tax liabilities do not accrue. However, as part of its marketing strategy the college may choose to use the trading company as a marketing vehicle itself and to market the college and trading company as having separate and distinct purposes.

Careful thought is required on the most appropriate company structure to be adopted and professional advice (both legal and financial) should be sought in order to ensure that the college company is properly established, accounted for and controlled and that the deed of covenant between the two bodies is correctly worded.

Incidentally, in drafting the marketing strategy, colleges should not lose sight of the fact that their new charitable status will make them potential recipients of charitable donations under deeds of covenant and gift aid arrangements where, in both cases, the value of the donation from a taxpayer can be increased through a reclaim of the income tax deducted on the payment.

Contract negotiation

Consideration also needs to be given to the process of contract negotiation within the college particularly in respect of the development of new business. Care should always be taken to ensure that any new contract signed on the college's behalf not only fits into the college strategy but is also properly drawn up.

The financial position of the college needs to be properly safeguarded in all contract negotiations and the college must ensure that appropriate contract review mechanisms are in place to provide this safeguard.

Ideally the college should have a series of standard contracts for the various types of services it is able to offer and should insist that these contracts are always used for new business. These standard contracts will contain clauses clearly spelling out the legal position of the contract, the financial arrangements and the taxation position (corporation tax, VAT) as well as the nature of the contract itself.

However, in practice some new business will be conducted in accordance with the standard contracts of outside bodies and the college needs to have an appropriate mechanism for satisfying management that such contracts are acceptable.

All contracts should be reviewed and signed by senior managers who will be responsible for certifying that appropriate checks have been carried out on the terms and conditions of the contract.

Conclusion

In the light of the competitiveness of the FE sector all colleges will need to establish an effective marketing strategy. Developments in the funding of further education will probably require colleges to be more financially independent thus making a marketing strategy doubly important.

The college's marketing strategy will be determined by its mission and objectives which in turn will enable an identification of a target market to take place.

Careful consideration is required to ensure that the college's marketing strategy is monitored and that all appropriate administrative and financial arrangements are made to ensure that the financial position of the college is safeguarded at all times.

Reference

Department of Education and Science *et al* (1987) **Higher education – meeting the challenge.** Cm 114 HMSO